The Hollow

Colossus

The Hollow Colossus

CHARLES ANDREWS

Needle Press

ISBN 978-0-9679905-4-5 (acid-free paper)
Needle Press / Oakland, California
Library of Congress Control Number: 2014952261

www.hollowcolossus.com

Preface

Working people enjoyed relative prosperity in the decades after World War Two, despite significant exceptions. Many a senior remembers good times then, but they have turned into insecurity and degraded employment today. This essay studies why.

The investigation looks into changes in the nature of work, the inevitability of economic slumps, and the subjugation of technological advance to the dictate of profit. The facts are readily observed, and the data are routine tallies. The challenge is to comprehend the historical path of capitalist accumulation and the barrier it hit. We find that two frequent themes of economic commentary, financialization and globalization, are superficial jumbles of description; the phenomena are effects more than causes. Our explanatory model uses a few propositions from the labor theory of value, but since they do not upset honest common sense, an exposition of the theory is unnecessary here.

Study foretells a different future, but only action makes it real. The principles of a new order call out: this we must do, we can do it, and it will be glorious.

Contents

1.

Production Advances
But Prosperity Recedes

Among the contradictions of capitalism are recessions, depressions, and slumps. The name varies, and so does the intensity, but they keep coming. One of the worst was the depression of 2008.[1] The number of employed people fell seven million in two years, doubling the unemployed count. Six years later, fewer people had jobs than in 2007.[2] Why did this happen? Something big is wrong when so many jobs disappear so fast.

Before the depression, 26 and a half million people received food stamps. The number climbed almost every month, reaching 46 and a half million people by June 2012.[3] Twenty million people and their families had not qualified for food assistance or did not want to apply for it. Now they had no other way to feed the children.

When people all around you lose their jobs, are you next? The wonders of a capitalist economy hit broad ranks of workers. One indicator is the earnings of employees in the private sector. In December 2007 they earned in total just under $87 billion a week. That amount fell to less than $80 billion at the start of 2010 (six months past the declared end of the recession). By June 2012 earnings approached $90 billion, a mere $3 billion above pre-recession Dec. 2007. However, because of inflation, real private sector earnings were still down $5 billion.[4]

Well-to-do commentators fill television and newspapers with praise of capitalism. They admit there was a recession, even a deep one. Sometimes they concede that there should be a safety net for people who have been dumped on the edge of survival. The difference between conservative and liberal talking heads comes down to how much government should do to help capitalism present a human face. The insistent claim, though, is that capitalism "rewards entrepreneurship and hard work, largely on the basis of markets and competition."[5] However, while the payoff for wheeling and dealing might be good, the reward for hard work has shrunk. This is the key fact that we must confront: *average hourly earnings in the private sector peaked in 1973.*[6] Income from work has stagnated and declined ever since. The American dream of a better life from generation to generation is over. Why did it happen and what can be done about it?

Much of the work comes in bits and pieces of a job. Average hours worked per week fell three hours from 1973 to 2007. On the other hand, someone who wants to keep a full-time job must work more hours than his parents. The percentage of nonagricultural workers who work 49 hours a week and more increased from one in seven in 1976 to one of every five employees in 2007.[7]

Employment / population ratio

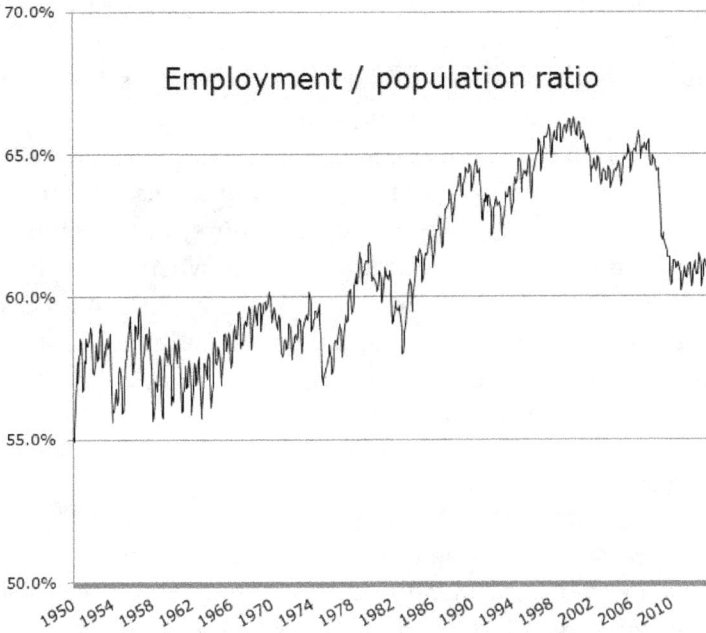

Recessions have changed, too. By one measure there were complete recoveries from the downturns that began in 1973, 1981, and 1990. A key ratio of economic vibrancy is the percentage of people, age 20 and over, who are employed. (See figure.[8]) In these three slumps, job losses pushed the ratio of employed people down. Three or four years later employment was back to its previous high point. The overall trend was more people working. These were the decades when women entered the workforce in large numbers.

The so-called dot-com bust of 2001 was different. The percentage of people with jobs fell and never fully recovered. The ratio of employed inched up for five years to the next peak, which was still below the previous one. Then the depression of 2008 revealed more fully the rot in the economy. The employment-population ratio collapsed almost five percentage points, and in the years since then, the ratio has stumbled along a depressed flat line. What will happen after the next crash?

The long-term trend of lower hourly wages after inflation, more precarious and onerous hours, and a shift of income from labor to capital (especially when we include in the latter outrageous "salaries," bonuses, and stock options for top executives) combined to reduce full-time workers' share of gross national product from one-third in 1979 to one-fourth in 2012.[9]

❖

Forty years of wage stagnation and decline, with no turnaround in sight, are historic. Real job earnings are a fundamental indication of how the economy performs for people. (Business profits are the crucial measure for corporate executives, Wall Street investment bankers, big stockholders, families of inherited riches, and other personifications of capital.) When real wages do not rise, there is a problem. If they fall and take five and even ten years to recover, the problem is serious, as everyone knew during the depression of the 1930s. Today we are in much more than one of the cycles of prosperity and depression that fit into a trend of increasing mass prosperity. That rocky ride characterized capitalism for almost 200 years.

The only contender for extended worsening of the reward for work might be a 25-year period within the first half of the nineteenth century in England; historians still debate whether it happened. That was when the modern working class was born and suffered hell in the new workplaces of industrial capitalism, steam-powered factories. The question today is whether capitalism is at its end.

Although real paycheck earnings are vital for the economic well-being of working people, they are not the entire sum of compensation. Many employers also pay in part for a retirement account and health coverage. About two-thirds of employees get a contribution to a private retirement plan, and employers pay into Social Security. Roughly similar figures apply for employer contributions to health coverage, and employers pay into Medicare for retirement. Health care when you need it and income during retirement are certainly vital needs. By and large, however, they are not regular expenditures during working years. The total cost to society of health care and pensions is growing. As we will see, the supplements do not relieve the decline in real earnings.

Later we will see how employers and financial firms took secure retirement away from workers. As for health coverage, employers paid more year after year because health insurance corporations, hospitals, and drug companies have been able to charge more. The price of health plans goes up about twice as fast as the general inflation rate. This was the setting for the Affordable Care Act ("Obamacare"), which most people will find raises cost or compels them to accept less care.

Real median earnings for employees fell from 1973 on, but not all individuals experienced the decline directly.*

---

* The median is the figure exactly in the middle when we list everyone's earnings from smallest to largest. It is the best single measure of typical earnings. In contrast, the average is what everyone would earn if the money were divided equally – but it is not.

For many, earnings do rise from their first full-time job until late in their life of work. The impact of the trend is that someone who started out in 1983 or 1993 or 2003 began from a lower level than those who began in 1973 – and moves through more jobs but less advancement in a lifetime of work. Many a family has a bittersweet experience when their child reaches young adulthood, realizing that she will never enjoy her parents' standard of living.

The decline of earnings appears as a gradual dimming of prosperity and comfort, punctuated by shattering economic blows to one group of working people then another. Not long after 1973 the industrial Midwest turned into the Rust Belt. Millions of factory workers in their 40s and 50s were tossed out the gate, forced to take Walmart-style jobs at drastically lower wages or driven into the idleness and penury of enforced early retirement.

The 2008 recession landed its strongest punch on a different group. Young adults trying to get a college education were hit hard. Total student loan debt rose rapidly and steadily even before 2008. From around $200 billion owed in 2000, it passed the one trillion dollar mark in 2013.[10] The recession confronted debt-burdened graduates with unemployment or a get-by job. Paying off the student loan became as burdensome as a house mortgage. Many participants in the Occupy Wall Street movement that rocked the United States in 2011 were caught in this vise.

❖

What caused an unprecedented 40-year decline in real earnings? The causes and conditions must have been in place before 1973 in order to produce an economic turn that year. Trends that swelled after that date cannot explain what began then. New things like globalization and the increasing dominance of financial capital amplify the basic development but did not cause it.

Closer to the facts are the consequences of technological change. It can certainly eliminate jobs. However, it is not a determining force by itself. Sometimes the condition of working people gets worse. Steam-powered looms invented two hundred years ago by Edmund Cartwright, William Horrocks, and Francis Cabot Lowell destroyed the livelihood of cottage weavers like William Carnegie, the father of Andrew Carnegie. Looms decimated hand weaving from 1820 to 1840. At the same time in England, landowners drove millions of farmers off the land. The new factories where the Industrial Revolution occurred exploited these first-generation workers terribly.

Once past the traumatic beginning of industrial capitalism, the main concern about machines and factories was not the decimation of farming, crafts, and work at home. The problems were in the jobs: brutal conditions in mills, endless hours, pitiful wages, and the dehumanizing effects of stupefying repetition. Certainly, companies failed and whole industries withered when new technologies destroyed them. The employees had to take care of themselves without social support; capitalist progress leaves a trail of destruction.

Still, the great crusade throughout industrial capitalism was the struggle of workers for a share of the new prosperity. They won it by bitter strikes, even open warfare, down to the anxiety of an individual employee asking his employer for another penny per hour. Wage increases were easier to win than shorter hours. In addition, it was almost impossible for the workforce to participate in the

15

design of jobs; capitalists knew that a big source of their wealth was to polarize the work so that most people did a few repetitive tasks that did not depend on individual skill, while managers and engineers structured and watched over the whole production process.

After World War Two automation became an issue. A notable social critic, joined by the public at large and some trade unionists, looked at it and foresaw a new attack on employment and wages. Fear of another depression like the slump of the 1930s probably heightened awareness of several technologies. In combination they were destined to raise the productiveness of labor enormously.

The critic was Norbert Wiener. He drove home the importance of the link between three technologies in his 1948 book, *Cybernetics: or Control and Communication in the Animal and the Machine*, and then in a popular rewrite, *The Human Use of Human Beings: Cybernetics and Society*, published in 1950 and revised in 1954. At one end were sensors that "feel" pressure or dampness, "hear" sound, "see" light and other electromagnetic waves, and measure a host of other conditions. They report changes through an electrical current or a mechanical movement. At the other end were machines, or devices added to machines, that could be switched by a relay to begin an action at a precise strength. The connecting link in the middle was electromechanical and pure electrical logic, which accepted sensor reports and decided what action to initiate.

To achieve automation, sensors measure the result of machine action, reporting back to the decision logic. The brain of the machine adjusts the action to stay on course. Wiener stressed the importance of the feedback, a general-

16

ization of hand-eye coordination. If you rule a straight line on a piece of paper then guide scissors along the line, the cut does not stay true by itself. Your eye and hand muscles must communicate and compute through your nerves and brain to get a reasonably straight edge.

Wiener was inspired not by scissors and paper but by the anti-aircraft problem of World War Two and the radar solution. He was contracted to work up some peripheral applied mathematics. Although Wiener's results were not used, his exposure to the project stimulated a general analysis of cybernetics.

With radar, British and U.S. artillery teams could shoot down German bombers by aiming cannons automatically. Reflected waves signals were fed into electromechanical analog computers, and they issued voltages to power trains, which positioned the artillery. Radar does not predict exactly; the figured position of the bomber a moment later is not quite correct. Using the next measured position as feedback, it was possible to calculate a more accurate aim, then fire the shell and hit the bomber.

The automated combination of radar and artillery helped smash the 1944 German V-1 "buzz bomb" offensive.[11] Although World War Two sped up technological development, the anti-aircraft solution relied on analog computing methods that electrical engineers had created in the late 1920s.[12]

In all these developments, electrical relays and vacuum tubes did the job. The transistor, destined to replace vacuum tubes, burst on the scene the same year as Wiener's first book, 1948, but semiconductors would need almost another decade to begin their amazing leaps of cutting size in half and doubling switching speed every two or three years. How many children today, given a tablet com-

17

puter in school, are told that one of the first microprocessor chips, the Intel 4004 announced in 1971, had 2,300 transistors, while the tablet in their hand has around 500,000,000? Yet Wiener foresaw enormous consequences when electronic "brains" were still made of vacuum tubes. Very few schoolchildren hear about his concerns.

Wiener feared that the development of automated machine systems would create "an unemployment situation, in comparison with which ... the depression of the thirties will seem a pleasant joke."[13] Things did not happen this way. Instead, the dividing line between unemployment and employment blurred over several decades. The 1950s hardly knew temporary employment through labor agencies (outside of farm workers), jobs where you wait for your employer to summon you for a shift of two hours or ten, and wages so low that employees qualify for food stamps. Nonetheless, Wiener glimpsed a new and fundamental decline of industrial labor.

❖

In 1957 the word "automation" appeared in books thirteen times more often than it had in 1952.[14] On the cinema front, Katherine Hepburn and Spencer Tracy starred in the 1957 movie *Desk Set*, which wrapped a romantic comedy around the threat that a large new computer might automate a staff of research librarians out of their jobs.

Hollywood chose a clean white collar occupation, but trade unions in this era represented blue collar workers for the most part. Automation was a serious problem for them. The economist Ben Seligman spent most of his career in academia but also a crucial period from 1956 to 1965 on the staff of the United Autoworkers and then the

Retail Clerks unions. His *Most Notorious Victory: Man in an Age of Automation* takes the reader close to a variety of new automated production setups.

In steel rolling mills, "sheets must move through rollers at high rates of speed. Variations in thickness must be detected quickly if a sheet is not to wrap itself around a roller."[15] Sensors connected to logic circuits took over control of the rollers. Faster operating speed and elimination of rework sped up output.

Even the steel oligopoly, noted for decades of technological stodginess, automated. "In Catskill, New York at U.S. Steel's captive Atlas Cement Division, fourteen old kilns were replaced with a single giant, 620 feet long, which was fully computer controlled."[16]

By the late 1950s and early 1960s, continuous processes were especially suited to automation with relatively simple computers. To make continuous rolls of paper in Fourdrinier machines (patented in France in 1807), the speed, temperature, composition of the pulp, and tension must be monitored and adjusted. A computer system at the Fitchburg Paper Company took over the observation and measurement, reading 90 instruments every three minutes, although adjustment was left to an operator given warnings by the computer.[17]

Another academic reported, "Employment in the increasingly automatic oil refining industry (which is highly unionized) has fallen from 147,000 to 137,000 since that time [1948], although refinery production rose 22% [by 1955]."[18]

An icon of the midcentury U.S., Wonder bread, was notorious for its airy consistency. Automation was introduced to measure the ingredients with photocells, combine them, slice the baked loaves (a feature advertised in television commercials as indeed a wonder), and wrap them. The cybernetic equipment reduced employees on affected sections of the line by 50 to 70 percent, with greater output per hour.[19]

"The meat packer can also use an automatic scanner that judges the fat content of bacon and guides the slicing knife, so that the resulting packages will have the same numbers of slices and the same weights." Camera images of the bacon traveled through a new material, glass fibers. The image detail was lost, but the light passed through a revolving disk with a slit onto a photocell, generating electrical signals in proportion to fat.[20]

A 1964 survey of 3,500 plants found that more than half used automatic sensors and control instruments.[21]

Automated production of relatively old-fashioned electronics parts was an ironic portent of the future. In 1961 Western Electric completed a computerized makeover of the manufacture of carbon resistors, those little plastic-encased cylinders that provide a definite amount of electrical resistance through a blend of conducting carbon and non-conducting ceramic. The many steps of making the core, capping it, welding leads, and packaging were now done without human action. Only a few workers watched instruments along the 120-foot line.[22]

"In 1951 only seven general-purpose digital machines were being used in manufacturing. Ten years later there were almost 7,500 such systems."[23]

An early, relatively simple instance of automation in the automobile industry is worth a closer look. When Ford Motor Company built the Brook Park engine plant in Cleveland, Ohio, one purpose was to help scatter the 60,000 workers at the River Rouge complex among factories across the Midwest. Each factory would employ no more than 3,000 workers in an effort to dissipate their militancy. The new plants opened the way for a hefty dose of automation, too. A machining line more than 1,200 feet long accepted a rough hunk of metal at one end, transferred it from one machine to another, and ejected a completed cylinder block at the other end. The line implemented feedback principles, measuring the block along the way and adjusting the machines accordingly. For every eight workers on the line before, Ford needed only one employee now.[24] In a "rocker arm support operation, five workers at two machines had produced 38 pieces per hour; after automation one worker produced 750 pieces per hour."[25]

The union members at Brook Park were angry about becoming more closely tied to a single huge line that insisted on attention at its own pace, that is, the pace that managers dialed in. The definition of job tasks, too, was a matter of struggle with Ford management, not a technical fact. And what would the jobs pay? The president of the local found that he had to conduct a sustained campaign to get the attention of United Auto Workers chief Walter Reuther and his colleagues. A series of wildcat strikes, each broader than the previous one, finally moved the national union. National and local officers negotiated job classifications and pay scales at Brook Park. The next national Ford contract had a more generous unemployment benefits program. These provisions offered some relief to current union members.

Then Reuther, as president of the Congress of Industrial Organizations (CIO), convened a National Conference on Automation in 1955. He accepted the conventional wisdom of economics professors that the long-term effect of automation would be wonderful for everyone, but government must cushion short-term blows to individuals. "We need to get down to a retraining program for our workers... We have to protect them during the interim period, during which the relocation and the retraining takes place."[26] Later he proposed a joint campaign with the automobile corporations to enact a national Manpower Development Training Act.

By 1958 Reuther was president instead of the industrial union department in the merged AFL-CIO. It convened a conference that year on "Automation and Major Technological Change: Collective Bargaining Problems." The subtitle was accurate: the speakers largely confined their practical urgings to collective bargaining clauses in line with experience at Ford Motor Company. Speeches ranged from concerned to complacent.

Speakers at the conference noted an important difference between automation and previous mechanizations of labor. Early machines tended to make skilled craft workers obsolete, but the takeoff of the industrial revolution created large numbers of jobs. In the middle of the industrial revolution, machinery ousted workers from some industries, but new industries employing the same general semiskilled labor arose. Now, automated machines eliminated large numbers of semiskilled jobs, and it was not clear that workers would find new industries beckoning to employ masses of them. Albert Whitehouse, director of the industrial union department, was pointed:

"Experts told us that any dislocations would be temporary and unimportant. They told us, if you will recall, that automation would create skilled jobs by the tens of thousands and that the new technology would bring higher wages for those it displaced... It is time to point out that automation and other major technological change have failed to bring automatically those things promised so blithely. Where are the great numbers of more highly skilled jobs?"[27]

Union officials did not demand public employment to work on social needs that capitalist enterprise ignored. They reached for a traditional pair of remedies: collective bargaining over the introduction of new machines and a call for greater overall demand (purchasing power) in the economy. Identification of automation as the economic problem subsided. Robert Heilbroner, an economist who wrote for the public, assented to complacency in the short term but warned of a problem after fifty years:

"No question is more important than that of the time span over which the technological transformation of society is apt to take place. The President's Commission on Automation has just completed a thoughtful (if near-sighted) investigation into the impact of automation over the next ten years and has reported that we have nothing to worry about in any fundamental sense. I do not quarrel with that conclusion with the span of another decade. Even at its very worst, technology is not like to create unemployment on a massive scale in so short a time, particularly if we follow the Commission's recommendations for the maintenance of a high level of demand... But what about another *fifty* years of change?... Sometime between ten and fifty years hence,... we must ... find some means of subjecting the technological invasion to responsible public control..."[28]

Heilbroner cast the problem on a time scale within capitalism. He did not question whether capitalism could cope with automation in its new form. His estimate of the time available to respond was too long, and the character of the problem turned out not to be mainly unemployment. Instead, workers' earnings peaked and fell into a long decline less than a decade after he wrote. "Responsible public control" was a mirage.

❖

Wiener labeled the forthcoming wave of automation a second industrial revolution. The first one took off with textile mills, and spawned one new industry after another. It advanced from steam-generated mechanical force transmitted along belts and rods to electrical power delivered through wires. It reached its crest with the metal-working and assembly lines of the automobile and appliance industries.

Automation is not really a second industrial revolution. The long run of industrialization, credited to the economic vigor of capitalism, changed around 1973 into its opposite. Automation is a technological aspect of capitalist *de*-industrialization. However, technology alone does not explain what happens in an economy. We need a few economic concepts, in particular the process of capital accumulation, which orthodox economists virtually forbid from being spoken.

Capitalists do not spur innovation and productiveness for their potential gift of plenty for all. Capitalist activity is governed by the mandates of accumulation, the expansion of capital value by the investment of profits.

Conventional economists have suppressed efforts at grasping economic change since the middle of the nineteenth century. They confine themselves to statics: the market runs like a mouse on a treadmill. The mouse is never hungry nor overfed, it never gets tired, and the treadmill axle never wears down. It is always a surprise when exceptional things happen; economists cobble together a one-time explanation. More or less official academic reviews of the discipline admit, "Toward the end of the nineteenth century, when economic analysis began more self-consciously to follow the precepts of scientific method, statics and dynamics were more rigidly compartmentalized. At first this meant in practice that systematic dynamic analysis was largely abandoned and was confined primarily to some casual observations about the time processes that underlay the well-developed static constructs."[29]

The statement is accurate, except for the babble about "the precepts of scientific method." In the latter nineteenth century economics consolidated its adherence to anti-scientific positivism. While official ideology acknowledges that there must be both statics and dynamics, its guardians insist, upon penalty of ostracism, that economists concentrate their theoretical attention on markets, the trading of goods and services, deeds of ownership and other contracts. "Exogenous" (coming out of the blue) technological events are allowed, too. With this approach, one can understand only the most superficial aspects of what drives changes in production and how they affect relationships between classes.

Capitalism – the reality, not the ideological fantasy – brings change through the gate of accumulation. In industrial capitalism, a dominant portion of all products sold on markets are produced for profit. The corporations, smaller firms, and other businesses run for profit have productive assets and employees. We call these producing organizations capitals.

Capitals reinvest a percentage of their profits. Now the money is part of the capital, expected to make more profit.

This is the accumulation of capital. It flows through various channels. Corporations reinvest in their business when it is profitable. When they pay back bonds with interest and pay dividends to shareholders, much of the money finds its way to other investments through financial intermediaries such as commercial banks, investment banks, and so on.

The goal of capital is not a steady level of profit but continually larger profit. This objective is enforced on each capital by the struggle among them. We can call it competition provided we understand that it is much more than price competition within a static industry. The law of capitalist competition is gobble up or be swallowed up. Profits are the weapon of combat.

Summed over the entire economy, new investments cannot be simple expansion, that is, production of more of the existing products by existing methods. In order to sell more of the same item, the seller generally needs to reduce the price. Accepting smaller margins for larger sales volume is not a viable long-term strategy. The cost of production must be reduced.

Some cost reduction can be achieved by economies of scale, the rough rule that up to a point each item is cheaper to produce when you make twice as many of them. Of greater importance are more economical methods of production based on new machinery. Such cost reduction is a weapon of struggle both within and between industries. Within an industry, the capital that can reduce price while maintaining profit margin takes sales away from competitors. Then they strive to catch up.

Cost reduction also permits the addition of new features to products without raising the price. The automobile did not change in a fundamental way in the latter half of the twentieth century. It remained a metal shell with rubber tires connected by axles to an internal combustion engine that burns gasoline or diesel. Simple cost reduction, shared at least in part with the buyer, would merely shrink the industry. Instead, by adopting new features like the automatic transmission in place of the manual gear shift, air conditioning, FM stereo in place of scratchy AM radios – all while holding the line on total cost in inflation-adjusted dollars – automobile companies kept up their share of the consumer dollar.

Lowering price and piling on features for the same price have their limits, too. People will not buy and store more than a certain number of pairs of socks, no matter how much the industry works to reduce the price per pair and no matter what variety of colors and textures it offers.

Accumulation drives capital to introduce wholly new products that take buyers' dollars away from existing ones. Capitals in one industry, often a new one, introduce products that make old ones obsolete. Word processors in the late 1970s not only replaced typewriters; the capability to format documents and use different typestyles upset the printing industry, too. Then personal computers and small printers attacked word processors. Wang, a major producer of the latter, fell from its throne. A short generation later, in the early years of the twenty-first century, so-called tablet computers and smartphones took away large chunks of the personal computer market, both desktop and laptop. They also established new markets among people who like a smartphone but had never found much use for a personal computer in the house.

A simple classification gives us an overview of the dynamic, disruptive nature of accumulation. Start from a baseline year. Some roster of products was produced:

bread, shirts, trains, and so on. Five years later, for example, there is a different roster: bread, different shirts, trains, and cars. The new roster, compared with the old list, divides into three sections: existing products produced by existing methods, existing products produced by new methods, and new products. The boundaries are not absolute, as shown by products that improve an existing one for the same or lower cost.

Innovative products lure sales revenue, but prospective buyers must give up something in order to purchase them. While an innovative product does something new, therefore, it must actively displace an existent product or products, fulfilling a general function in a cheaper or better way. Television shrank attendance at movie theaters as well as newspaper readership. The shift in purchases may be broader; we want a television, so we buy less expensive clothing.

Accumulation occurs by redistributing output among the three sections. Although some existing products made by existing methods may be produced in larger volume, this section shrinks overall under attack by capitals that accumulate in the second and third sections. Existing products made by new methods may be produced in larger or smaller volume than previously. The output of innovative products obviously increases from zero.

Accumulation thus generates a series of industries in overlapping arcs of birth, growth, maturity, and contraction.

❖

Setting aside the products themselves for a moment, let us consider the work of the people who make them. When the roster of products changes, labor must be redistributed. Let us assume that the labor force is a fixed size in order to see what happens without the complication of a growing population. Reduced output of existent products ousts labor from the sites of their production, while new products require workers to make them. The redistribution of labor is essentially costless for capital. Workers no longer needed are laid off. Where new workers are needed, plenty of applicants show up. Occasional shortages and geographic shifts might require minor expense to overcome. Workers go to where the jobs are, not vice versa (except when a capitalist relocates to where wages are exceptionally low).

Certain characteristics of industrial labor enable its redistribution to go smoothly. Considering any one job, a large percentage of the workforce can perform it. A newly hired employee needs a few days of training and two or three weeks to get "up to speed." The work is broken down into the simplest motions, the most rigid rules of procedure, and the most basic tasks of attention, memory, and action. The worker's job consists of repeating a dozen or two such operations again and again.

Jobs are confined to routine, repeatable functions that can be performed with modest variation of efficiency from one worker to the next. The worker receives inputs, crunches them in a pattern that can be represented as an algorithm, and performs an action as his or her output. The input is through the senses, noting clearly defined qualities. Has the color changed? Has the bin filled? The input can also be data like a number read off a meter. The algorithm performed in the worker's brain is comprised of simple arithmetic, lookups in a short memorized table, and application of well-defined if-then rules. The output is muscular actions or the issuance of a number or item of data, whether written down, spoken, or selected by the hand moving a switch or a lever.

Strictly excluded from industrial labor are mulling over disparate observations as much as needed until one can conceive a solution to a problem; making judgments based on vague and ambiguous information; and collective consideration of larger goals and social priorities in deciding what to do.

Capitalist industrial production consists of routinized labor working at machines. Industries differ from each other more in what their machines do than in the mass of workers who tend them. Capitalist reutilized labor replaced medieval skilled craft work. That work had required a long apprenticeship to develop coordination of hand and eye; intimate knowledge of variations in clay, wood, or fiber; keen observation that drew on experience to know when a process like baking was done; the sensibility to imagine a specific shirt, brew of beer, or watch; and the know-how to produce it. The bulk of capitalists are driven to employ routinized labor for the mass production of standardized products.

By the late nineteenth century, workers were raised in factory-like elementary schools, which extended slowly over the decades into high school and community colleges. In 1909 Woodrow Wilson was president of Princeton University. He told a group of high school teachers, "We want one class to have a liberal education. We want another class, a very much larger class of necessity, to forego the privilege of a liberal education and fit themselves to perform specific difficult manual tasks."[30] His remark is clever. Wilson first states candidly that a large working class must forego a privilege; then he misrepresents their work as "specific difficult manual tasks," which really means repeated, alienated, dull, draining tasks and endless suffocation of the human spirit.

We will call it standard labor.

Such has been most of the labor in capitalist industrial production. It can easily be redistributed among industries, making possible what accumulation must have: new products and new methods of production. "Constant revolution of production, uninterrupted disturbance of all social conditions, everlasting uncertainty and agitation distinguish the bourgeois epoch from all earlier ones."[31]

❖

Where does capital find innovative products and new methods of production? They are born out of discovery, investigation, invention, and development. New realms of nature are discovered. Processes operating there are investigated. Devices are invented. They are engineered into more or less reliable, easily used products that can be manufactured on a large scale.

It is not a neat four steps. People boiled steam from water for millennia before a handful of Englishmen, James Watt being the most well known today, combined the simple act with metallurgical knowledge, also known for a long time, to make steam engines. Heron of Alexandria in the first century CE grasped the practical physics of containing steam in a sturdy vessel and releasing it in one direction to create mechanical motion. He made a metal sphere rotate on an axis by boiling water in it and discharging the steam out attached bent tubes. Scientist Robert Boyle, son of the Earl of Cork, raised the theoretical understanding of gases about a hundred years before Watt's work on the steam engine, but so far as we know,

31

Watt did not use Boyle's laws of gas pressure and volume. Theoretical understanding of heat in a body and its conversion to mechanical power came later.

Watt was both inventor and commercializing entrepreneur, an exceptional combination. Usually, the inventor does not know how to hack a safe path through the business jungle. He loses his invention to businessmen who commercialize it for their profit, not his.

Discovery and invention are dramatic moments, but much more time goes into investigating a new realm of the material world and developing a new contraption into a series of practical things. During two hundred years of capitalist industrialization, 1750-1950, scientific investigation and the engineering of new products became more closely connected with each other. Early on, a scientist was a wealthy dilettante, a self-educated man, or a bright apprentice. As understanding of matter and its motions became deeper and more intricate, it necessarily divided into specialties focusing on a particular realm like mechanics, chemistry, or electricity. Scientists and engineers required four or more years of higher education in preparation to enter an organized profession with societies, journals, and sometimes licenses recognized by statute.

Toward the end of the nineteenth century, several large corporations in post-mechanical, pre-electronic industries started their own laboratories: Kodak in photography, B.F. Goodrich in rubber, General Electric in electricity, followed by du Pont in chemicals, the Bell Telephone System, then dozens more. Once in awhile ambitious engineers and scientists start a company in a new industry and grow it into a big corporation, as Hewlett and Packard did with instruments and then electronic calculators, computers, and inkjet printers. Still, in 1950 there were only 182,000 scientists and engineers among 60 million civilian employed in the United States.[32]

The two professions swelled from 1950. Somewhere around 1963 the number of employed scientists and engineers passed the one million mark. While increases remained high over the rest of the twentieth century, the rate of growth subsided. In 2007 there were six and half million scientists and engineers, four percent of employed civilians.

At the heights of science people design experiments that compel nature to answer crucial questions. Pondering a jumble of facts, which may present an outright paradox, they discern a necessary process that can be grasped in laws and equations. The critical experiment compels matter to answer whether a theory holds, or at least is not false, while proving other hypotheses false. Such an experiment is so noble that it has a Latin name, *experimentum crucis*, originating from Francis Bacon, Robert Hooke, and Newton when scientists still wrote books like *Novum Organum* – New Instrument – in a dead language.

Most engineers and scientists do much less high-level science. The work of science-derived innovation, as well as much of the knowledge that fuels it, is largely trial and error experiment and calculation on more or less well-established equations, catalyzed with doses of the ingenuity that formerly established a new industry without much science at all. A professor of industrial management said, "Put some scientists in a well-equipped laboratory, pay them a fixed salary and they will invent or come up with new ideas at a predictable rate."[33]

Scientists and engineers perform what we will call scientific-technical labor. Under capitalism it pulls in oppo-

33

site directions, toward broad knowledge but also to immediate use for profit.

The science conducted by the most devoted practitioners, people who search for deep truths, drives to comprehend the essence of things. Material essence has three aspects. First, it is the process of something. That is, science proposes explanations of how a realm of matter moves, displaying the phenomena we observe. Second, the motion is both how a thing exists and its journey of transformation into something else. Third, science proceeds on the general rule, never broken yet, that things are inexhaustible in their content. Matter yields some of its secrets now, but we will learn more later.

The goal of a technical enterprise, however, is a specific new power of transforming matter or an advance of productiveness in a specific activity. In 1816 Jacob Bigelow coined the term "technology" to mean "the application of the sciences to the useful arts."[34] His definition is not quite complete, since investigation of nature by trial and error for a specific productive purpose may precede the relevant science, spurring development of the latter. Plant breeding stimulated evolutionary and genetic science. In contrast to the three aspects of essence, technology is interested in one or two effects of the motion of matter; it cares about larger change mostly to forestall it from disturbing a repeatable production process; and it ignores the inexhaustible potential of things beyond its narrow goal of the moment.

Still, the difference from science is not antagonistic in general. Science, after all, is practical, too – but it has a wider vision of what may become practical. The belief is warranted that all knowledge of the world eventually helps humankind do better at production and communication and stewardship of nature.

Under capitalism, though, science and technology are in contradiction. Capital invests in new knowledge of matter not for eventual usefulness, but for the immediate gain of the investing capital. The product is useful only as needed to sell it and make a profit. Capital tries to ignore all other consequences.

The Marxist philosopher Georg Lukács discussed the immediate and more far-reaching goals of scientific knowledge: "If the result of the experiment is to be used to improve the labor process, there is nothing problematic about practice as a criterion for theory." The test of practice can be fairly narrow to solve a narrow problem, but things are different when science aims at "expansion and deepening of our knowledge of nature in general. In cases such as this, a merely mathematical grasp of the quantitative aspects of a material relationship is no longer sufficient; the phenomenon must rather be comprehended in the real specificity of its material being, and its essence as thus comprehended must be brought into agreement with other modes of being that have already been established scientifically."[35]

Lukács does not reject quantitative knowledge in tandem with attention to all aspects of being. His contrast of the mathematical-technical and the deeper being of things is roughly parallel to the contrast between routinized wage labor and craft labor, as well as the contrast between production for profit disdainful of pollution and production regulated for the well-being of the community and nature.

Industrial production repeats the production process again and again, relying on predictable results under specified conditions. This feature is analogous to scientific

35

law, which states what must happen given specified conditions. Every time they are met, the outcome verifies the law; the experiment can be replicated. Replication in technology becomes repetitive production in application.*

❖

Capital in its search for profitable innovations in the 1950s drew on broad reservoirs in the sciences. Computers depended most immediately on semiconductor and ferromagnetic physics, information theory, and mathematical logic, but automation utilized results from chemistry, metallurgy, other branches of materials science, and more. Scientific-technical innovation eliminated standard labor in existing industries and founded new industries that need little of it.

Innovation did not become purely science-based. Industrial engineering, an ancient process by comparison, continued to oust semiskilled workers from their jobs. The freight railroads carried almost the same amount of cargo in 1960 as they did in 1950; ton-miles fell three percent, tons 8 percent. Employment, though, plummeted from 1,237,000 to 793,000, a drop of 36 percent. This was the decade when the diesel locomotive became powerful and efficient enough to wipe out steam locomotives. In 1950 the railroad corporations had 27,000 steam locomotives;

---

* Scientists need not replicate a process to establish truth. Science requires verification, which may be achieved by other means. Geological study, for example, discovers and establishes the history of the earth. However, we do not replicate the earth the way it was billions of years ago then watch it form tectonic plates and continents again.

36

in 1960, only 374. The 15,000 diesel locomotives in service in 1950 doubled by 1960.[36]

Diesel engines had been known since the late nineteenth century. Engineering improved them at a relatively slow industrial pace. After the delay of World War Two, railroads began rapid investment in diesel locomotives. They require less maintenance than steam engines, and they do not need to refuel as often. Ton-miles per railroad employee increased 52 percent over the decade.[37]

Computers helped railroads schedule traffic and use equipment more efficiently. However, while jobs dropped by 444,000 in the 1950s, which was the decade of the diesel, employment fell less than half that number in the 1960s, the decade of railroad computerization.[38]

The results of materials science are relatively unglamorous compared with computer science and medicine, for example, and its theory is less dramatic than physics. Yet innovation in materials enabled advances in a wide swath of technologies. Ceramics were known for thousands of years and their chemistry gradually understood over the last 200 years in bricks, tiles, toilets, and dinnerware. That changed in the middle of the twentieth century. "In 1950, nearly all of the articles published in the Journal of the American Ceramic Society were industry related; by 1960 only a minority of articles were related to commercial product manufacture or use."[39] Ceramics were applied outside the old clay industries. They helped make possible spark plugs, catalytic devices in oil refineries as well as the catalytic converters in automobiles, packaging for fragile slices of semiconductor silicon, separators in rechargeable batteries, replacement parts inside the human body, and superconductors.

We have lacquered and treated wood for millennia not only to give it a gloss but also to strengthen and protect it. Plywood – thin layers of wood glued together, usually at cross angle for strength – proved to be a major innovation to the same end. Although ancient Egypt and China made approximate predecessors, and although nineteenth century investigators and engineers invented machines for the manufacture of modern plywood, a good waterproof adhesive was created in the 1930s. Wartime and postwar technological development pushed the strength and adjustable qualities of resin binders to a new level.[40]

The variety of plastics, long atomic chains of organic molecules assembled by chemical procedures, multiplied. Acrylic was used where glass was too fragile or costly. Plastic wrap was more flexible than paper and transparent, too. Mylar plastic film was invented in an industrial laboratory and patented in 1952; it was an elaboration of the basic chemical from which nylon is made.

Cardboard combined with a thin layer of polyethylene plastic and sometimes aluminum could replace glass bottles with milk and juice containers that do not leak. Today there is often more science-based technology embodied in the box than the contents. The ketchup bottle changed more than the ketchup, at least until the arrival of genetically modified tomatoes in the 1990s.

A branch of plastics chemistry was crucial to a major change in electronics labor. Radios, television sets, oscilloscopes, various instruments, mainframe computers, telephone equipment, and amplifiers consist of complicated circuits. Many vacuum tubes, later transistors, were wired to each other and to resistors and capacitors. The assembly job had been reserved for decades to women. "By the late 1920s, there were 6,000 women but only 400 men employed by U.S. factories making tubes, radio receivers, speakers, capacitors, and transmitters... A survey taken in 1953 ... showed that nearly all workers on television assembly lines were women. These women (used) hand tools to do repetitive tasks such as wiring, soldering, lacing the wiring in TV sets, inserting parts in sequence, inserting tubes, and final testing."[41] Help-wanted ads in newspapers were categorized between men and women. Under the latter heading, a typical 1956 ad placed by Burroughs in Pasadena sought to hire "Electronic Wire & Solder Girls."[42]

As electronics output rose rapidly, the printed circuit board replaced the increasingly intricate maze of wires. Electrical paths were etched from a layer of conductive metal fused to the substrate. Modern printed circuit boards would not exist without the epoxy resins from which the board is made. Scientists in Germany, Switzerland, and the U.S. had invented epoxy resin in the 1930s. The resin sets hard, can be mixed with fiberglass for an exceptionally strong but thin board, and will bond to a metallic layer.

The printed circuit board eliminated the work of tying wires to components and threading them correctly from one lead to another. An engineer drew the logic of connections, then a machine printed it on boards. The leads of components were placed into holes, at first by hand, later by machines. Soldering at the hole was simpler manual work. At a Philco plant in Sandusky, Ohio the change to printed circuit boards eliminated a quarter of the workers on the soldering and wiring line. Then wave soldering replaced most of this work, too. The board is placed over a pan of hot solder, which is given a jerk to send a wave of solder just along the bottom of the board, setting all the joints at once. At the Philco factory, wave soldering cut the number of solderers from 40 to three.[43]

Certainly, the semiconductor gets prime credit for enabling vast output of electronic devices, but we should not overlook the contribution of the printed circuit board. Together, they explain how electronics became a major industry without generating semiskilled industrial jobs on the scale of automobiles and other appliances.

Titanium is more common in the crust of the earth than copper, tungsten, and zinc, but it was not produced in volume as a metal until the 1950s. The compound titanium dioxide, which provides an opaque white base for paints and pigments, began mass production in 1916 in Norway and Niagara Falls, New York.[44] The next step, reducing titanium ore to a metal, was a challenge. DuPont and other companies, enjoying scientific-technical spadework by a lone inventor in the 1930s and scale-up research by the U.S. Bureau of Mines, entered production of titanium. Output of sponge metal went from 68 tons in 1950 to 6,710 tons in 1955.[45]

Titanium is an expensive metal, about ten times more costly per pound than aluminum, and costly to machine. It is used when a part must be exceptionally strong, operate at high temperature, and resist gas and salt water corrosion. More than half the output goes into aircraft, both at crucial junctures of the frame and in engine parts. Titanium is also used in petroleum refineries, papermaking, steam turbines in power plants, and the acid-holding vessels and pipes of chemical plants. No account need be taken of titanium golf clubs and eyeglass frames. Because of the high cost of titanium and the engineering work needed to put it to best use, its presence in equipment is testimony that a growing portion of fixed cost outlays, real investment in other words, goes into research and development.

Capital allocated an increasing percentage of investment funds to scientific-technical effort not because capitalists are enthusiastic about science but because it was necessary. Back in 1945 Vannevar Bush, a leading manager of science on behalf of capital, prepared a report on the topic. He started from the reality, "Today ... basic research is the pacemaker of technological progress. In the nineteenth century, Yankee mechanical ingenuity, building largely upon the basic discoveries of European scientists, could greatly advance the technical arts. Now the situation is different." He called on the federal government to pay for basic research, while recommending that corporations enjoy "deductibility of research and development expenditures as current charges against net income, and ... strengthening the patent system..."[46]

❖

The new technology of the 1950s was not exclusively the fruit of high-level science. Teams conducting methodical but not especially profound experiments produced much of the underlying knowledge. They did the same thing in principle as a single craftsperson feeling her way to the recipe for a new pottery glaze. The difference is one of scale; university, corporate, and government laboratories run many trials at once. To be sure, the bit of science that pointed the way to promising results was more advanced than what crafts and industry had in the past.

We tend to overemphasize automation among the scientific and technical changes of the twentieth century, and the computational part of automation over the sensor inputs and the implementing actions. One reason we do this is because of a cultural primacy of ideas over matter, including formal logic over material action.

The real importance of the sense-calculate-respond model lies in its application to both machine action and standard labor, enhancing the former and demeaning the latter. Like a machine, standard labor receives inputs through the senses, computes, and performs a response (a muscular set of motions, which may be a "real" motion or be a symbol that the worker writes, speaks, punches on a keypad, or taps on a touch screen. Mass production needs the algorithmic model in order to be reliably repetitive.

The model provides a framework for machines to replace workers. New sensors, more powerful computers, and refined machine actions fit into it. Until capitalists propose that a worker must submit to bioengineering before he gets a job, there are physiological limits on the functions of standard labor. A person can only distinguish so many colors, feel pressures within certain limits and to a certain degree of precision; the worker can only remember so many style codes; she can perform very intricate motions, but the arms and fingers do have limits of delicacy. Although we can work longer and more intensely than people a century ago, although we are taller (and lately, fatter), we are basically the same physiological human beings that we have been for thousands of years. There are limits to what sense organs, nerves, and muscle can do. This is especially true when standard labor is specified in detail, which is the basis of every mass production process.

At the beginning of industrial capitalism, mechanization ousted workers, the skilled in particular, from their jobs. Nonetheless, new industries generated work for standard labor. The brute muscle toil of the ditch digger was eliminated, for example, but factory work provided jobs that demanded rapid motions.

Around the middle of the twentieth century, new industries *from their beginning* do not require much standard labor to produce their products. Whatever tasks the industry needs performed, equipment based on scientific-technical development is soon at hand to do them.

The signature change was the maturity of automobile and appliance industries, which shaped pieces of metal and assembled them on factory lines. Electronics, particularly integrated circuits on semiconductors, displaced them as growth industries. "Detroit," the capital of the industrial Midwest, had hired millions of factory workers who made automobiles and the steel, rubber, and glass parts that went into them. Electronics, from transistor radios to calculators, through a host of industrial equipment unknown to most of us, to personal computers, digital cameras, cellphones and then smartphones, did not create replacement jobs of standard labor at anything like the same numbers. The capital of this industrial complex is "Silicon Valley," a collection of campus-like development centers in a small area around San Jose, California. "Detroit" extended to neighboring states; Silicon Valley is one section of the comparatively small San Francisco Bay Area.*

Semiconductors are baked by the millions in fabrication plants requiring a handful of workers. The key to their mass production is their small and continually

---

* The same contrast with Detroit applies to Silicon Valley's early rival, Route 128 around Boston, which enjoyed brief hegemony in the minicomputer era.

shrinking size, enabling so many of them to be printed on a thin wafer of silicon. But what about the rest of the production process? In the early days, women put the semiconductors into ceramic or plastic packages and soldered gold wires to the chip. Within a few years, even looking through a microscope a worker could not target the tiny solder locations. It was necessary to create robots that could assemble semiconductor packages. Scientific-technical powers were great enough that such machines were designed and built. Long before tedious soldering could swell into a significant number of industrial jobs, the work was automated.

Electronics resembles the old industries only in the final step of production. The circuit board, display, power module, perhaps a disk drive and a keypad, must be assembled into the housing of a desktop computer, laptop, or trendy tablet from a corporation named after a fruit. The assembly phase did rely on standard labor. A coincidental event gave manual assembly work a lease on life. Vast pools of cheap standard labor became available in China, the former Soviet Union, and eastern Europe after 1989. Standard labor held off automation with wages a tenth or less of the pay in the United States and western Europe.

After twenty years or so, wages in China started to rise (although still a mere fraction of U.S. pay). Automation attacks those jobs, too. Foxconn, the contract manufacturer of electronics products that employs more than a million workers, most of them in China, announced in 2012 that it would replace employees with a million robots in the next five years.[47] The following year, the government of Zhejiang Province said it would "invest" $80 billion over five years to equip manufacturers with robots "to over-

44

come the short supply and high cost of labor." The average labor cost in 2012 was 41,000 renminbi ($6,700) in the province, implying that firms can amortize the cost of a robot in three or four years.[48] A Chinese market research-er estimates the country will install 45,000 robots in 2014 and triple that number per year by 2020.[49] (A robot may replace several workers.) Foxconn later admitted that its forecast was exaggerated, but robots will oust a large amount of standard labor from the assembly of electronic devices.

We will return later to globalization, showing that, real as it is, it is not the cause of the degradation of industrial labor.

Standard labor is expelled but has no productive place to go. The redistribution of labor is upset. A compar-atively small cadre of scientists and engineers create new industries that simply do not need much of it. As Norbert Wiener feared, science-based automation and other inno-vation bring the industrial use of standard labor to its his-torical end.

❖

We can now summarize in a qualitative way two phases of capitalism – the industrial and the scientific-technical.

Industrial capitalism exploited standard labor. Work-ers, by organizing, using the strike weapon and the threat of it, and campaigning for legislation that set limits on ex-ploitation, extracted some of the gains of increasing pro-ductiveness. They ate better, lived in more comfortable homes, enjoyed modern transportation in cities and be-tween them, and kept up with a new global network of in-formation (which began 150 years before the Internet with the telegraph, cross-country mail via train, and printing presses that could flood a city with newspapers several times a day).

Disruptive accumulation compelled the redistribution of labor through recurrent cycles of boom and bust. In times of prosperity, new industries might need to offer higher than average wages because established industries were going strong, too. During slumps, the more outmoded industries and less efficient companies shut down or laid off a good portion of their workers.

For all the alienation of assembly line and related labor, workers discovered their collective strength at the heart of accumulation. Most jobs offered little sense of craft pride, yet workers could discuss where society was going and what their rightful participation should be. However, pay, safety, and benefits were the main topics of bargaining. Struggle over control of the production process was largely about the pace of work and the pay differentials among jobs that management defined.

The capitalist passage from industrial economy to a crippled scientific-technical era poses a new challenge. Now the normal course of economic advance ousts workers from their jobs without fully taking them up in the forefront lines of new production. A new economy struggles to be born. Genuine progress must be discovered by deep analysis of decay, wresting the positive from the negative. We must understand the new problems of accumulation, innovation, and the redistribution of labor.

❖

Let us review how occupations shifted from 1950 to 2000.

When Norbert Wiener voiced fear about the imminent arrival of automation, operatives, laborers, and craftsmen were 40 percent of the employed. Also in 1950, one of every eight persons in the workforce did farm work. (See Table 1 at end for this discussion.) How quickly would these occupations contract, and what would replace them?

By the year 2000, agricultural work occupied less than one percent of the workforce. The classic blue-collar categories were still substantial at 24 percent of the employed, but their proportion had fallen sharply from 40 percent.* Clerks, now called office and administrative support workers, gained a net increase of three persons per one hundred in the workforce. Clerks might be necessary for production of goods and services. They support purely financial activity, too.

Clerical jobs grew from twelve to eighteen percent of the workforce in 1970, then fell back to 15.4 percent of employed people by 2000. Desktop computers, computerized small-scale printers, and local area networks marched like Sherman's army through the ranks of office work.

---

* The Census had revamped occupational categories, too. The table groups old and new slots for approximate comparison. Occupations, like a list of specific types of products (what Karl Marx called use values), do not remain identical over time. The Census Bureau does not try to illustrate fundamental change. It prefers a distribution of categories in reasonable proportion to each other and gussied up with ideological names. We can nevertheless see large, important changes through a clouded lens.

The biggest growth of an occupational category was in so-called professional and related occupations, more than doubling from nine to twenty percent over the 50 years. These 26 million jobs bear a closer look. We already noted the growth of scientists and engineers required for innovation; there were almost five million of them among the 130 million people in the workforce in 2000.[50]

The two largest areas of the category are education and healthcare, comprising more than half the professional and related jobs. The notable fact is the capitalist imperative as they grew to make them commodities that "customers" obtain through private purchase, choosing the quality level they can afford. What kind of society educates people to the level their parents can buy? What kind of society decides whether to treat an injury or a disease according to the financial means of the patient?

In the industrial era, capitalists accepted a mixture of equality and privilege in elementary education. They needed semiskilled workers with basic literacy. Higher education was a certification of privilege as much as truly advanced learning. In the first part of the scientific-technical era, 1950-1970, it seemed that higher education would be partially democratized. College education expanded dramatically. The children of middle-income families had opportunities to become the needed scientists and engineers as well as educators and such.

Healthcare grew, too, with one foot in capitalist markets and one foot outside them. Health coverage through the employer was a component of the employment market. Medicare for people 65 and over, enacted in 1965, was financed not by individual purchase but through socialized funds collected and disbursed by government. In other industrial countries the social funding model extended to most of the population.

Although our analysis of occupation stops at 2000, we all know that capitalism has taken aim at the large education and healthcare sectors. From Microsoft multibillionaire Bill Gates to the equally wealthy clan of Walmart founder Sam Walton, big capitalists demand that education become a pure commodity. Under the cover of vouchers for a few poor families, they want it to be purchased more and more by individual payment and tiered to match an increasingly polar distribution of incomes. Education conducted by communities with more or less progressive public funding must be destroyed.

Healthcare grew in a peculiar way that could not last. Health insurers, hospital chains, and pharmaceutical corporations enjoyed the lucrative rewards of operating with minimal price competition. That era is over. As the population separates into rich and poor, the former will buy the care that modern science makes possible, but the latter cannot afford it, so the healthcare industries must fashion a health care counterpart to fast food for the masses.

Corporate executives across the economy agree that people should have less health care for the money. They want most people to buy health coverage individually, with or without money from the employer to help pay. Controversy over government health programs comes down to the same demand. The so-called Tea Party Republicans start from the unstated premise that private health care and private health insurance are the only option. President Obama's program served capital in a different way. It applied the power of the state to subsidize corporate health insurance and health providers, commanding everyone to buy insurance.

How about a plan like the original Medicare, extended to all ages? It could relegate private insurers to a minor role and clamp down on the profiteering of health care capital. Too uncapitalistic.

Health businesses have converted most doctors into employees told to cut corners. Hospital administrators said Dr. Janis Finer needed to see 22 to 28 patients a day. "At one point, we were scheduled to see patients every 11 minutes," Finer said.[51] Physicians are offered more pay for prescribing either less care than needed (when the patient is on a flat premium plan) or more care than needed (when the hospital can bill for an operation). Registered nurses are pushed to follow instructions from a computer.

The numerical growth of professional and related occupations in the twentieth century was not the increase of an unchanged category. The more people in these jobs, the more the jobs lost their relative charm.

Education and healthcare are entry industries into a new economy. A scientific-technical economy needs more education than an industrial economy. A sliver of the workforce must be scientists and engineers; that is a demand of accumulation. Under capitalism, though, the vast ranks of standard labor are not to be admitted to a new economy. They scratch on with declining earnings or they drop into long-term unemployment.

Another occupational growth area was jobs in management, business, and financial operations. We assume that scientific-technical work does not require more managers, more business dealers, and more financial manipulation than did auto and steel, for example, in the industrial era. The growth of the category is an outcome of capitalism trying to cope with the problems of crippled accumulation. The same is true of another growing occupational category, sales. Business got along fine in 1950 when these two broad categories employed sixteen of every one hundred people in the workforce. Now they take up 25 of every one hundred employees. At the top end of the income scale, the managers and sales stars are the best at playing an unproductive game. At the low end of the scale, vast numbers of people are cashiers and retail sales workers on the floor, trying to get by in what has been an employers' labor market since 1973.

The last occupational category for our examination is the most formless: service jobs. They almost doubled from 7.5 percent of all positions in 1950 to just under 15 percent in 2000.* Four out of ten service jobs are janitors, personal care services, and such. This is a growth of jobs while capitalism stagnates, not the development of human productive powers. Indeed, much janitorial work could be automated (think of robot vacuum cleaners made rugged), but it does not pay to automate the lowest-paying jobs.

Almost another third of service workers prepare food. The conversion of housewives into part of the general economic workforce spurred a parallel conversion of meals into commodities. The declining earnings of workers overall, and the increased hours that families must give employers, are reflected in the rapid growth of fast food outlets in the middle of the twentieth century.

Norbert Wiener's dire prediction of massive unemployment in the absence of massive government action did not materialize. Instead, the occupational changes of the last half of the twentieth century reveal an economy una-

---

* This analysis examines occupations. Statements that the majority of jobs are in services, especially in contrast to manufacturing, are based on classification by industry.

ble to accomplish the revolution from industrial to scientific-technical production.

❖

The 25 years after World War Two are called the Golden Age of the U.S. economy. The 1950s, following a postwar recession and before the distortions of the Vietnam war, was its peak decade. Incomes rose, and jobs were plentiful by capitalist standard. Two brief, shallow downturns were among the mildest of the century. A considerable number of young people entered careers their parents had not dreamed of.* Earlier we surveyed the scientific-technical innovations of the time. Yet an examination of employment in manufacturing industries, the heart of industrial labor, shows the gestating change.

Manufacturing jobs increased from 1950 to 1960, although not as rapidly as employment in other sectors the economy. In fact, the number of manufacturing jobs in a growing workforce climbed until 1979. During the 1950s, manufacturing added 1.5 million jobs.[52]

The Census Bureau breaks the jobs into two categories, production workers and all the others. Production workers include what the term suggests, plus maintenance persons, janitors, and clerks who keep records at factories and other production sites. Working supervisors are included. Nonproduction personnel are the managers, technical staff, sales staff, lawyers, and so on.[53]

---

* Great blotches marred the shiny picture: the educational and economic segregation of Black people, the shacks of rural, coal-plundered Appalachia, and factory fields of lettuce, fruits, and cotton in California and the Southwest.

During the 1950s, *all* the increase of manufacturing employment was nonproduction jobs (except for a miniscule 39,000 production jobs). We will presume, without examining the change in products produced, that manufacturing output in 1960 was larger than in 1950. The sector processed the food that fed more people, made their clothes, and produced their vehicles and appliances. By the end of the decade, the same number of production workers with modernized equipment produced a much greater volume of output.

Manufacturing industries needed more nonproduction jobs, or at least companies found it paid to add them. More engineers and technicians worked out how to replace old machines with the new ones. No doubt jobs were added in sales and management, too; the firms could afford to hire them, and their activity enabled the corporation to make more money.

The shrinkage of production jobs and the hiring of nonproduction employees to implement technological advance becomes more evident if we examine particular industries within manufacture. Fifteen industries defined by the Census Bureau account for most manufacturing employment (86 percent). The pattern of new jobs during the 1950s is revealed when we sort the industries by rate of job growth. (See Table 2 at end.) The fastest expansion was in more science-based industries: electrical equipment, which included such electronics as radios, televisions, communications equipment, and electronic components; instruments; and transportation equipment except motor vehicles (essentially, aircraft). These three industries also saw their proportion of production workers, already below the level for all manufacturing, fall more rapidly than average. They depended more on employees who design and develop new products.

On the other hand, the three industries that lost jobs were textile mills, lumber products except furniture, and motor vehicles. The auto industry was a special case at this time, a fat oligopoly just beginning to meet consumers' resistance to bloated, chrome-laden cars that changed superficial appearance every year like ladies' fashions. Textile and lumber went through less technological change than average during the decade, and their percentages of nonproduction workers were among the very lowest.

❖

In the early 1960s observers of these trends could justify a complacent or a concerned attitude. The complacent view was that manufacture remained strong and expansive even as it became a smaller percentage of growing employment. Technological change opened new job opportunities. Observing a less rosy scene, a few trade union officials and labor activists sensed a deep problem, asking whether new and more human forms of work were assured after "temporary dislocation." It was probably too early to foresee that the endless drive of capital to accumulate and hence to adopt innovations would now occur without creating new industries of mass employment. It would have been especially difficult to go beyond observations to a compelling demonstration that it would necessarily happen.

One man who identified a problem was a hero of industrial trade unionism, Wyndham Mortimer. The auto workers' triumph in the 1930s was a mass achievement, but he was the one person who did more to make it happen than anyone else. A coal miner's son, Mortimer put in countless hours building the auto union, starting from his World War One days operating a drill press and organizing a union at White Motor Company in Cleveland, to his dispatch as a lone organizer to Flint, Michigan. When he arrived, the auto union there had only 150 members, yet it was only six months before the great sitdown strike began on December 20, 1936. Mortimer went on to fierce struggles for a militant line in the national UAW, and then to more successful organizing in southern California aircraft plants.

In the mid-1960s Mortimer wrote in retirement, "Time was when we could expect new industries to take up the slack, and the men and women displaced in one industry could eventually find work in another. This is no longer true. It is not true because investment capital is not being plowed back into new industries in America in anything like the amount required to employ the millions now being displaced by automation. When investments are made, it is in automated plants and factories where fewer workers, not more, are employed."[54] Mortimer identified this fact as the threshold of solving the problem of millennia, "the problem of how to produce in abundance for all." He saw far beyond the trade union and liberal focus on Keynesian full employment policies and government aid to retrain workers for new occupations.[55] Mortimer was a communist in outlook as well as a dedicated, far-seeing, hardworking union organizer. Therefore, his warning went unpublished for years.

Some prominent social critics of the day took note of change in the nature of work and of new sources of innovation, but they did not analyze how capital accumulation responded to emerging productive powers. Herbert Marcu-

55

se, who wrote the best-selling book *One Dimensional Man*, interpreted automation and its fruits as absorbing the working class in a pleasantly oppressive system. Michael Harrington in his best-seller, *The Other America*, documented and dramatized how the prosperity of the day had not reached a significant percentage of people. He did not question the economic trajectory of capitalism. Indeed, his book was an appeal that capital could easily afford to include the excluded. In reality, Black people fought for civil rights, largely achieved them, then found themselves tumbled into even worse economic situations. Corporations and government did co-opt an extremely small elite for comfortable positions of service to capitalism.

Marcuse allowed himself to be celebrated as the grandfather of the flower children of the 1960s in place of profound radicalism. As for Harrington, when it came time to take a basic stand on the war in Vietnam, he voiced qualms about U.S. policy but said in 1965, "I am anti-communist on principle because I am pro-freedom."[56] In other words, the Vietnamese people may march for a better life and be shot dead on a Saigon street, but in no case would he support their war for independence from the United States and the increasingly vicious puppet governments that it maintained.

Industrial labor was exhausting and mind-numbing, but at least it was part of economic advance. The masses could obtain a share of prosperity. Today a majority of working people must take jobs that are not part of a new economy, except when new means worse. Broad forward motion to a better life has disappeared. Our task is to understand why.

2.

Their Analysis and Ours

Three commonly asserted causes of our economic troubles are technology, financialization, and globalization. Explanations based on them include some valid description; otherwise, they would have little traction. Yet when we look at their logic and the evidence, they fall apart.

Regarding technology, Ray Dalio has an answer for us. He runs what is said to be the largest hedge fund, the $150 billion Bridgewater Associates. Dalio must have a view of how the entire economy operates, and it attracts investors when he pontificates. After a bad year for his funds, he needed to boost his credentials, so he gave Charlie Rose an interview in early 2014. One of their exchanges went like this:

Rose: "The president has been talking a lot about income inequality. What's your take?"

Dalio: "I think it's mostly a function of technology. Higher productivity means you don't need people the same way you did before. And it will be a much bigger issue going forward... People – from a business point of view – are machines that do things. And now they can not only physically but intellectually be replicated with technologies, and that has an effect on the demand for labor."[57]

Dalio certainly is blunt about the grim fate of workers. He presumes the domination of capital with no concern for the situation of human beings. However, he explains too much. More productive machines have displaced workers for 250 years, yet much of the time the working class extracted better wages.

As for taking over intellectual action, machines did it long before modern computers. The steam-powered loom wove fabric from thread in the eighteenth century, but if you wanted more than the simplest pattern, you had to buy hand-woven cloth. Joseph Marie Jacquard invented a system of punched cards in 1801 that guided power looms to weave intricate designs. It was as amazing then as intellectual replication is today.

Overall, Dalio's summary does not support a conclusion about the demand for labor. He glides over the question of how vigorously the accumulation of capital generates new jobs, and therefore the wage that capital might be willing to pay to fill them. The problems are income inequality and the decline of wage earnings; explaining them from technology alone is a short circuit.

A 1990 report from the high-powered Commission on the Skills of the American Workforce conveyed a tone unlike Dalio's, one of social concern urging policies that would make capitalism work for people (actually, vice versa). Yet the commission's reasoning about technological causes was equally defective. It recognized what was at that point a twelve percent fall in real average weekly earnings since 1969, admitting, "This burden has been shared unequally. The incomes of our top 30 percent of earners increased while those of the other 70 percent spiraled downward." The commission tossed out a bit of history. "The steam engine and the electric motor drove the first two industrial revolutions, causing profound changes in work organization. This boosted productivity, quality, and living standards dramatically." Supposedly, when work caught up and re-organized according to the imperatives of new technology, living standards rose. Now, says the commission, we are in a "third industrial revolution" heralded by "the advent of the computer, high speed communication and universal education." If workers will conform to the new organization of work, their earnings will rise, not fall.[58]

The mainstream commission of policy advisors could not inquire into how investment decides which new technology to bring in and when, in subservience to the god of profit.

The title of the commission's report posed "America's Choice: high skills or low wages!" Get those skills, and you can fit into the new pattern of work. Not quite. The commission distorted the typical understanding of skill. After interviewing managers at hundreds of companies, the commission admitted, "Few talked about the kinds of skills acquired in schools. The primary concern of more than 80 percent of employers was finding workers with a good work ethic."[59] To be blunt, workers must drive themselves more intensely. "Management layers disappear as front-line workers assume responsibility for many of the tasks – from quality control to production scheduling – that others used to do."[60]

The commission then wrapped its admonition in layers of talk about skill as we usually understand it, asking for the public to choose how to divide job training costs among individual workers, government and business.

The workforce commission, like Mr. Dalio, began with shoddy allusions to technology as the determinant of our lives in the hope that an aura of inevitability would cover its class conclusions.

It is no surprise that new methods of production ("technology") affect the relationship between the exploiters and the exploited. The fruits of labor come into being at the point of production. In capitalism workers do not earn a wage unless they work, they cannot work without the necessary equipment and facilities, and they work with them only when they sell their labor power to the owners of the means of production. Naturally, the output belongs to them, too.

Technological change happens within the relations of production. If we begin from this reality, we are open to discover the most basic problems confronting an economic order. Dalio, the Skills Commission, and other apologists for capitalism cripple their analysis of stagnant real wages, widening inequality and other problems. They take technology to be an independent, largely non-economic stream of events that affect the economy. At best, superficial observations about markets and technology are allowed. Such narrow vision is unable to explain the degradation of labor for 40 years and more.

If technology shaking things up unpredictably is not the cause of our troubles, what about the second of the three major candidate explanations?

❖

"Financialization" refers to the rapid growth of financial paper and a faster pace of trading it, especially in comparison with the total output of manufactures, crops, and more or less real services. The term appeared in books a few times in the 1980s, became more frequent from the early 1990s, and spread more rapidly from 1998 on.[61] At the Library of Congress, the first book with the word in the title arrived in 2002, *The Financialization of Daily Life* by Randy Martin.

There are three broad categories of financial paper. Equities are claims of ownership on a business or on assets like machines, buildings, and even the right to use a patented technical process or a copyrighted brand name. The business or asset is supposed to produce a flow of profits; equity paper establishes a legal right to the profit. Equity pieces of paper are typically called shares or stock. Since the force of the paper is a construct of property relations, not a quality of the embossed certificate, the latter was replaced successively by records on magnetic tapes, hard drives, memory chips, CDs and such. Profits are distributed to the equity holders, typically as dividends.

The second category is debt, a claim to receive a defined stream of money payments (interest) and periodic or final repayment of the principal, that is, the money or valuable item originally given the debtor in exchange for the paper. Typical names for this paper are loans, bonds, and notes. The debt may or may not be secured by collateral, something the creditor can petition a court to seize if the debtor fails to make a payment on time.

The third category, derivatives, is distilled from the first two. A derivative is a contract created with an initial payment in return for a right to future proceeds related in some way to a flow of equity profits or debt interest and principal. In addition to centuries-old options and futures, derivatives include the credit default swaps and collateralized mortgage obligations that became famous when they collapsed in 2008. Derivative can be piled on top of derivative in equity, debt, and further derivative form. Derivatives shade into gambling bets between two parties, wagers about whether a price of real stuff or, more likely, the price of a financial paper or an index based on a group of papers or real assets, will rise or fall a set amount by a specified date. Derivatives are more potent than plain equity and debt in their potential to reap huge reward (and suffer huge loss) and to threaten sudden economic disaster.

Financial leverage can be set up with ordinary debt. The financier puts up a little of his own money while borrowing most of the funds at a fixed interest rate to make a large bet. It would be wonderful to have the exaggerated returns of leverage without the risk it brings. Enter derivatives. In the 1990s, Wall Street traders and two Nobel-prize economists at a hedge fund named Long Term Capital Management claimed that with derivatives they could balance or "hedge" bets against each other to eliminate the risk while guaranteeing a profit. They gave investors in their fund returns of more than 40 percent in 1995 and 1996, after raking off more than a quarter of the profits for themselves. Managers of pension funds and college endowments, banks, and wealthy individuals ready to hand over the minimum $10 million investment piled in. LTCM was worth more than $125 billion "on paper," as the phrase goes. Then interest rates moved in a way the Nobel economists' spreadsheets did not permit them to move.

LTCM tottered at the edge of bankruptcy. Government authorities deemed the fund too big to fail; big banks might go bankrupt if their LTCM holdings were wiped out. A bailout was organized.

Speculative bubbles that end in sudden collapse, often but not always triggering a recession in the entire economy, have happened for hundreds of years. After the LTCM incident, the relevant federal regulator proposed that unlisted trading in derivatives needed some rules and sunshine. Deputy Treasury secretary Larry Summers denounced her, saying that the mere suggestion "cast the shadow of regulatory uncertainty over an otherwise thriving market – raising risks for the stability and competitiveness of American derivative trading."[62] Summers did not fear financialization; he promoted it. Federal Reserve chief Alan Greenspan welcomed it, too. So did Summers' boss, Robert Rubin. He glided between the post of Treasury secretary and an executive slot at Citicorp where he was paid around $126 million in cash and stock for his ten years there.[63]

Speculation turned to the stock market, where a "dot-com" bubble grew and burst in 2000. Soon a much larger bubble in home mortgages followed. Big banks and Wall Street bond dealers created and sold vast mountains of mortgage paper and derivatives built on them. It seemed that housing prices would rise forever. If a buyer did not have enough income to pay off a mortgage, so what? When he could not keep up the payments, he would sell the house, repay the loan, keep a profit, and buy the next one. So it seemed until the collapse of a major Wall Street practitioner of financialization. Lehman Brothers went bust in September 2008, months after it was apparent that the housing bubble was running out of steam. The entire stock market crashed, too, falling more than 50 percent.

The financial crisis let everyone know that a severe depression had begun, although it is usually called the Great Recession of 2008. As economic data became available, the National Bureau of Economic Research decided that the downturn had started in December 2007. As this essay is written several years later, the stock market has recovered, house construction has resumed, but unemployment remains high and family incomes have not recovered.

Despite his goon-style defense of derivatives from mild regulation, Larry Summers went on to become head of newly elected President Obama's National Economic Council. Washington shoveled money to banks deemed too big to fail. That might suggest breaking them up, but it was not done. The regulatory legislation that eventually passed is widely seen as insufficient. Meanwhile, General Motors was rescued on the backs of its workers, who took wage cuts and reduced health coverage. Twenty thousand retired workers at Delphi, a GM parts supplier, lost 30 to 70 percent of their pension.[64]

The blasé federal welcome of financial recklessness stands in contrast to corrective action during the great depression of the 1930s. Two days after Franklin D. Roosevelt became president, he shut down every bank in the country. The banks reopened with government assistance if they were deemed basically sound. Congress passed legislation that created the Federal Deposit Insurance Corporation (FDIC). The same Glass-Steagall Banking Reform Act forbid investments and speculation by deposit-taking banks. Basically, they must hold the loans they make, may not bundle and sell them, and remain responsible for collecting the payments. Investment banks became separate firms under the law, forbidden to combine in a holding company with a deposit-taking institution.

Roosevelt also created emergency work for people in the Civilian Conservation Corps and the Works Progress Administration. He enacted Social Security and reluctantly accepted federal rules allowing workers to form trade unions.

There was economic space for New Deal politics. Industrialization in and around the automobile industry had room left to run. Mass production of durable consumer goods like refrigerators had only begun. The consequences of radio, air transportation, and plastics were unknown but obviously a field of development. Capitalism could find a path out of the depression.

The question was, how quickly, and would people give it time? Millions of jobless workers, ruined farmers, and youth facing dismal prospects began to doubt the wisdom of subordinating production to the dictates of profit. The New Deal allayed just enough of their doubts, although Roosevelt's initiatives only softened the privations of the great depression. Unemployment remained high until the munitions buildup for World War Two began. Sometimes a capitalist government can deal with financial speculation. It cannot prevent depressions. At best it applies a balm while society waits for the economy to heal.

❖

Derivatives and speculation in general do not play a major economic role in ordinary times. Their moment of stardom arrives when a financial panic breaks out. Our concern is with the massive and prolonged growth of financial paper.

It may be measured by an increase of ordinary equity and debt. Was financialization a fundamental cause of the long-term decline of real wages?

Adding up corporate equities at their market prices and expressing the total in relation to the total income of private industry, we find that equities began a long rise in the mid-1980s. Furthermore, the starting point was from the depths of a steep fall in equities in the early 1970s. The ratio of total equity prices to private industry income only passed a 1968 high of 1.42 in 1995 when it reached 1.52. Equities swelled to a high of 2.68 in 1999. After that, despite gyrations up and down, they have never fallen below 1.52, except for the panic year of 2008. Equity financialization arrived a decade *after* the 1973 turning point, and it swelled and ebbed more erratically than the downtrend of real labor earnings.[65]

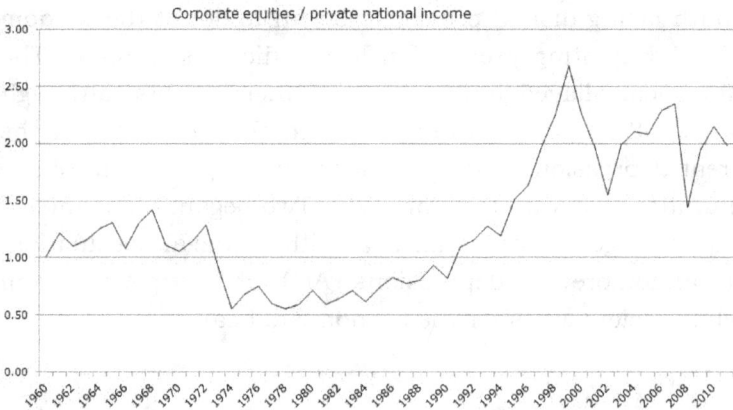

Corporate equities / private national income

Debt is more broadly based, measuring it as all nonfinancial debt in relation to gross domestic product (GDP). The debt-to-GDP ratio was 1.38 in 1960, and it fluctuated narrowly between 1.37 and 1.41 until 1981. From 1982 the ratio rose steadily, with only the smallest of occasional pauses and dips, to a high of 2.57 in 2012.[66]

The debt includes household mortgages, vehicle loans, credit cards, and other personal obligations; all the bonds and borrowing by nonfinancial businesses; and government debt. The increase was broad based. Here are the shifting percentages of the debt that each category of debtor owed:

Debt Outstanding	1960	2012
Household	29.8%	32.3%
Nonfinancial business	27.7%	31.6%
Federal government	32.5%	28.7%
State and local government	10.0%	7.4%
Total	100%	100%

Government debt grew less rapidly than the debt of households and businesses. There is a difference between the latter two. While the debt of nonfinancial corporations grew, so too did their income from financial paper; the nonfinancial corporation, still classified as a car manufacturer or whatever, made more of its money in the form of interest in particular.[67]

Another measure of financialization is the share of all corporate profits that the finance, insurance and real estate sector (FIRE) captured. Its share fluctuated around a mild uptrend from 1950 to 1980. Then in 1984 the percentage of profits taken by the FIRE sector began a steep increase until it reached an amazing high of more than 45 percent in 2001.[68]

When we survey the growth of equity paper prices, the weight of debt, and sectoral shares of corporate profits, we find that financialization took off from early 1980s. This is a decade after the degradation of standard labor began its long decline. Financialization cannot be the cause of something that began before its notable rise.

❖

So-called neoliberalism dates from the early 1980s, too. The term refers to both policies and ideology.

The policies include keeping hands off corporations when they cheat customers, oppress employees, or ruin communities and environments ("deregulation"). Neoliberals also want to dismantle, step by step if necessary, Social Security, education and anything else that capital does not directly own ("privatization").

Neoliberal ideology blesses the policies by preaching that unregulated markets achieve the best possible economic result and that government programs for working people are always bad. (Neoliberalism avoids talking about government welfare for corporations, such as tax loopholes and subsidies for research, for locating a factory here or there, and for other normal business activities.)

Did financialization lead to neoliberalism, or the other way around? Since both of them took off in the early 1980s, the question is secondary when we want to know what caused the fundamental problems of capitalist accumulation from 1973 on.

In the United States, however, progressive-sounding politicians in the Democratic Party like to blame neoliberalism for our troubles, claiming to be opponents of it. Actually, the first neoliberal president in substance, but not in strident ideology, was a Democrat. Jimmy Carter served the term before Ronald Reagan was elected in 1980. (Margaret Thatcher, an even more forceful proponent of neoliberalism, had become prime minister of Britain only a year and a half before Reagan became president.) Carter ran for President in 1976 by attacking federal "bureaucracy," but he sounded liberal themes, too. Once elected, Carter presided over deregulation of the airlines and of unionized long-haul trucking. He enacted a regressive, trickle-up tax "reform" in 1978. Carter appointed Federal Reserve chairman Paul Volcker, who fought inflation by pushing interest rates sky-high, deliberately engineering a recession. "The standard of living of the average American has to decline," Volcker said, turning a statement of fact that had been in effect for six years into a plan of action. President Carter did not object.[69]

❖

The long dismantling of secure retirement pensions is an illuminating slice of financial history. At the center is the Employee Retirement Income Security Act of 1974 (ERISA). At that time seven out of ten participants in a pension plan had a defined benefit: they would receive a guaranteed amount every month, based on a table of their years at work and their wage history.[70]

The spark for ERISA was the failure of the Studebaker-Packard automobile company. When it shut down its Indiana factory at the end of 1973, the pension fund did not have enough money. Current retirees got their monthly checks, but thousands of workers who had paid into the plan for years were given a lump sum if they were lucky, an amount much less than the worth of the promised pension over their expected lifespan.

Reformers and union officials seized on the event for legislation. While they concentrated on shoring up defined benefit (DB) plans, ERISA was more significant in the long run for paving the way to the vast expansion of a different retirement vehicle, defined contribution (DC) accounts, also called individual retirement accounts. The company puts a specified amount of money every pay period, month or quarter into an account for each worker. We know the accounts by the mystical numbers 401(k), 403(k), and so on, which refer to sections of the tax code. Because the account is subject to the vagaries of investment for decades, the employee has no assurance of how large the account will be when she retires and what she will be able to withdraw each month.

The trade group for mutual funds assigned a young lawyer on its staff to lobby on ERISA. In his book *The Rise of Mutual Funds: An Insider's View*, Matthew P. Fink boasts, "ERISA enacted the mutual fund industry's *entire* wish list."[71] Fink concentrated on defined contribution plans; tax advantages for Individual Retirement Accounts (IRAs); and the "investment" of account money in mutual funds, and therefore a limitless array of stocks and bonds and other financial paper, rather than being limited to insurance annuities. Fink was also able to make sure that mutual fund operators like Fidelity Investments bore no fiduciary responsibility to accountholders.

Employers steadily moved out of defined benefit obligations. Reliable figures begin with the enactment of ERISA. In 2011 four out of five people who had any pension arrangement had a defined contribution account.[72] Trade unions did not have the clout to prevent the exodus from defined benefits. The new pattern of capitalist accumulation undermined standard labor and its power in the job market.

Still, the percentage of pension assets in defined contribution plans barely shifted for the first eight years after ERISA was passed. DC plans had 29 percent of the assets in 1975 and 30 percent in 1983.[73] In order to promote IRAs, more tax legislation was passed in 1978, and the Internal Revenue Service took another year or two to issue regulations. Only then did 401(k) plans take off.

Finally, mutual fund operators could lure people busy at their jobs to buy funds with the money in their defined contribution accounts. In the eight years from 1983 to 1991, defined contribution assets jumped from 30 percent to 43 percent of the total. Most people at work do not have time to become knowledgeable market players regardless of whether they are speculators or so-called patient investors. They are lured and pushed into buying mutual funds in order to "keep up with inflation" and "allocate their assets."

In 1984 mutual fund assets of $117 billion equaled only three percent of GDP, the same as in 1960. Assets shot up to nine percent of GDP by 1987, and in 1999 they stood at 30 percent, at which level they have fluctuated until today.[74] The rise of these paper assets is an upside-down measure of the insecurity of retirement. Now it depends on the prices of stocks and bonds, which suffer wild fluctuations at unpredictable intervals. Tens of millions of people have become bitterly aware that their retirement fund may be slashed a quarter to a third almost overnight.

Financialization, taken simply as the spread of paper "assets," spread like a weed after a new economic situation weakened labor and left capital with fewer opportunities for investment requiring mass employment. Then legislation and deregulation dismantled old barriers.

Similarly, the exorbitant interest charges and fees on credit cards, payday loans, advances on income tax refunds, and student loans show up as revenue for financial capital. People are driven to these recourses because they cannot get by on their current earnings and do not earn enough to accumulate meaningful savings. What appear as financial profits are an outcome of the long-term decline in real earnings at the end of the capitalist industrial era.

Financialization is a consequence of our troubles, making them worse, but it is not their cause. What about the third of the three major candidate explanations?

❖

Another great "-ization" of our time is globalization. It is certainly real, but what is it? In a vague sense, it means that the regions and countries knit more dense connections around the globe.

Globalization today is more than international trade that increases faster than world output. Exports and imports have become more important to countries for centuries. There have been interruptions and declines, so that by one measure, globalization of trade declined from the mid-1920s to the end of World War Two. World trade did not grow markedly faster after the war than before.[75]

The countries of western Europe and Japan increased their share of world output in the 1950s and 1960s. At first, exports to the United States were not a serious issue; it was only an arithmetic fact that the U.S. supplied a falling percentage of the total output of the group. Later, certain industries like motor vehicles were hit hard. The U.S. share of manufacturing fell from 62 percent in 1950 to 43 percent in 1975. Japan's share increased from 2 percent to 13 percent, Germany's from 10 percent to 17 percent, and France and Italy nibbled a few more percentage points.[76]

Industrialization moved rapidly in these countries after World War Two. They were at the height of building automobile and appliance industries. Despite their gains in comparison with the U.S., the basic problem that we examine in the U.S. context hit these economies in the early 1970s, too. Annual growth of GDP in western Europe registered a stunning 4.8 percent from 1950 to 1973 then fell off a cliff to 2.1 percent in the next twenty-one years.[77] The growth of real wages in manufacturing also dropped from 1973. In the industrialized countries of the Organisation for Economic Cooperation and Development, the average wage growth rate of 4.4 percent in 1966-1973 fell to 1.5 percent in 1974-82 and 0.8 percent in 1983-1992.[78]

U.S. capitalism is more decadent than capitalism in other developed countries (except perhaps Britain), but accumulation started to break down in all of them around 1973. We must find the common motion of accumulation in developed capitalism. It is incomplete logic if one holds that the global economic shifts from 1950 to 1973 explain U.S. decline while ignoring the same problem in the other countries.[79]

Nor is it convincing to argue that when competition between capitals expanded to global scope, it caused long-term, apparently irresolvable troubles for accumulation in all the developed countries.[80] It is nothing new that one capital or another introduces new products or new production methods, takes the lead, and compels other capitals to catch up or die. Realignments are painful for many people, and capitals try to postpone writeoffs of dead investment. Still, vulnerable capitals shrivel, some capitals renovate, and some capitals develop new industries. This has been the story throughout the evolution of capitalism.

Compare an earlier geographic enlargement of competition. After the Civil War in the U.S, some markets expanded from small regions to continental scale – a consequence of the development of mass production industries and railroads. A new level of fixed investment in production complexes poured out huge volumes of output. Competition among nationwide producers was not the cause of the industrial changes. Nor did nationwide competition bring capitalism to an impasse. Instead, new productive forces inaugurated a hundred years of industrial oligopoly.

In any event, the current wave of globalization began after the rapid postwar growth of Europe and Japan. It is different in how it is done, its driving force, and its locations.

❖

At the core of the new globalization are worldwide chains of production controlled by one corporation, usually the one with its brand stamped on the final product. Your mobile phone might have been designed in California or Korea; the semiconductors baked in Taiwan; the glass cover over the display manufactured in upstate New York; and the device assembled in China. It was flown to your country, and the final leg of transport might be by truck, mule, or camel. The manufacturers in the production chain did not trade with each other on world markets; each firm worked under the master corporation that sub-

74

contracted one step of production to it. Such is the globalization we examine here.

Previously, world trade moved ores and crops that had a natural basis of specialization. Or a country built a manufacturing industry on machinery and skills of a new type before other countries. Today capital goes global largely in search of cheaper labor. The most blatant form is outsourcing: a corporation closes a factory in the United States and gets its output from Mexico or China. The firm uses the same technology as it had at home, except when wages are so low that more primitive methods are cheaper. Walmart demands lower prices from suppliers. It tells small and medium manufacturing companies that they must close their U.S. shop and move to China. Walmart accounted for 9 percent of all U.S. imports from China in 2006.[81] Manufacturing jobs disappear in the U.S., and the country has a trade deficit in manufactured goods.

Is globalization the fundamental cause of the erosion of good jobs in the United States? The history of the U.S. trade deficit in manufactured goods shows that this globalization arrived years *after* the decline of standard labor was underway. From 1967 to 1982 the trade balance in goods bounced between surpluses and deficits of less than one percent of GDP.[82] The latter year was the turning point, but the decline in real earnings had begun almost a decade earlier. In 1983 the deficit in goods hit 1.3 percent of GDP. Since then the U.S. trade balance has worsened over two broad cycles, hitting almost five percent of GDP in 2005. Considering that manufacturing generated 13 percent of the value in the economy that year, the trade deficit in goods is huge.[83]

The two countries most closely involved in the globalization that hits United States workers are Mexico and

China. As late as 1997, the U.S. trade deficit with Mexico was one-fifth of one percent of GDP.[84] NAFTA, the North American Free Trade Agreement, had gone into effect in 1994. The trade deficit in goods increased steadily to half a percent of GDP in 2013. Imports were 1.7 percent of GDP, which is a truer measure of outsourcing; goods exports to Mexico were 1.4 percent of GDP, which includes parts and kits to be assembled into final products, then imported back to the U.S.

China is a bigger story. Imports of merchandise grew from one-third of one percent in 1980 to 2.6 percent of U.S. GDP in 2013. The deficit in U.S.-China merchandise trade is lopsided; imports from China were 3.8 times U.S. exports.[85]

The role of China must be divided into two parts. Low-tech exports like umbrellas, shoes, and cheap furniture are largely based on cheap wages. The cost of the components does not overwhelm the value that Chinese labor adds. High-tech exports are different. Chinese assembly labor adds only a small part to the value of iPhones and other digital electronics. Most of the value comes from semiconductors that Japanese, Taiwanese, German, and U.S. corporations supply, and the fabrication plants may be located in places like Singapore, too.

Political events in 1989 and 1991 opened lush new pastures for global capital. Millions of Beijing workers, including many from government offices, went into the streets in the former year, angry about inflation and corruption. We are taught about the event as the Tiananmen Square massacre of students. The real significance of the student protest is that it opened a gate for the wider movement. Most students left the Square before the government overcame a tactical problem. It had difficulty finding army units who would drive tanks over unarmed Chinese people and mow down rows of demonstrators with point-blank rifle fire. The military killed several thousand city residents, almost all of them well outside Tiananmen Square.[86]

From that time forward, the Chinese government sped up capitalist economic development, including an open door for multinational capital and its local intermediaries. In effect, the regime told the population to forget about socialism. Each individual was welcome to scramble after the prosperity that a few would snare.

Also in 1989, the Berlin wall fell, marking the end of the German Democratic Republic; the country was formally integrated into West Germany within a year. In 1991 the Soviet Union formally collapsed after decades of stagnation since its 1956 turn away from socialist development. Criminal plunderers of state assets (the so-called oligarchs), capital from western Europe, and U.S. corporations rushed in to grab state-owned factories and hire cheap labor.

Looking back today, 59 percent of Russians interviewed in an opinion poll stated that Soviet socialism had more positive than negative aspects. Forty-seven percent of young adults, age 18 to 30, hold the favorable view, too.[87] Wide swaths of Chinese people lament that everything today in their country is about chasing money.

Apple Corporation, Walmart, and other U.S. corporations are attracted to China and Mexico for low wages, supplemented by greater freedom to release toxic chemicals into the air, rivers and ground. Still, they found these bonanzas almost twenty years *after* the peak of U.S. wages. A deep problem in the U.S. economy constitutes the connection between the sweatshop oppression of workers in industrializing China and the desperate jobs of greeters at Walmart in the United States. The real question is, what blocks the U.S. economy from moving displaced workers at home to better jobs? Why is capital now incapable of and uninterested in creating new sectors that employ masses?

Suppose events made it impossible for U.S. capital to contract production to China. As recently as 2010 the possibility was inadmissible: China needs U.S. markets as much as U.S. capital wants to employ cheap labor in China. By 2013, the foreign policy atmosphere had flipped. China is now a country in search of secure, cheap raw materials as well as outlets for investment. An early sign of its expansionary imperative is the belligerence toward neighboring countries over who will take oil and gas out of the South and East China Seas. Conflicts of interest intensify between the world economic powers.

If turmoil led workers to overthrow capitalism in the United States, what would replace all those imported goods? In the short run, a vast number of jobless people would be hired. They could produce exports for international trade on terms of equal labor exchange, as well as replacement goods in the United States. In the medium run, automation would be the answer.

Cheap global labor helps put off a wide range of feasible automated production. Industrial jobs get a lease on life – at the lowest wages. As noted earlier, though, contract assembly corporations are already moving to displace labor in China with robots. The U.S. caught up with Britain and surpassed it in the nineteenth century; then another half century of industrialization beckoned. Vast areas are now industrializing, but the old connection with mass prosperity is largely broken. China, for example, sets a record for rapid capitalist industrialization. Two or three decades from now, the country will likely arrive at the same impasse as the U.S. – an economy in which technology advances but economic, social, and cultural life regresses. Capitalism after industrialization is unable to achieve vigorous, profitable accumulation in combination with an improving standard of living.*

Neither new technology taken as an independent external cause nor rampant financial activity nor capital's feast on new pools of global labor caused the deep, permanent erosion of relative prosperity in the United States since 1973 and in other capitalist countries soon after. It is time to get past defective, apologetic, and reformist analyses of capitalism today to a scientific explanation. We need to acquire proper tools of understanding.

❖

The accumulation of capital requires innovation. We observed that automation and related innovations reduced the employment of standard labor in large industries like the automobile complex, while new industries based on

---

* To date, China has created a white-collar, professional, and businessperson layer of perhaps a quarter of the working population. In addition, many peasants have become factory, construction, and transport workers. Most of them are migrant workers, second-class citizens in the cities where they work. They fight sweatshop pay levels and working conditions, but the future is post-industrial and murky. As for the former Soviet Union, it was much less agricultural, more industrial and more white-collar than China when it fell apart. Life has become worse with practically none of the advances that make a mixed scene of China.

semiconductors and digital technologies do not employ many workers. Unlike financialization and globalization, the content of scientific-technical work in innovation increased dramatically in the decades before the 1973 turning point, not after. The observations suggest that we investigate accumulation more closely.

The key to accumulation in the industrial era is found in a stark expression of capitalist exploitation and irrationality – the cycle of prosperity and slump. Why must prosperity periodically end with a crash or other relatively sudden slowdown? Work disappears. People suffer unemployment and hunger because the economy gives them no way out for months and years. It does not happen because of a poor harvest or a huge storm. Something is defective in the economic relationships within which we live.

The cycle is inherent in industrial capitalism; no policies of any government have ever overcome it. If we see how both phases of prosperity and their cyclical breakdown are part of industrial capitalism, we may discover what is different when capitalism enters the era of crippled scientific-technical advance.

We lay out a model of how accumulation proceeds during the prosperity phase in order to circle in on the contradiction within that kills it more or less suddenly. The model assumes that all production during the previous year is stored and sold on January 1 for use in the new year. The choice of a year is arbitrary. Output consists of consumption goods and instruments of production. We assume that all stored production is for use in the year. This includes the instruments of production; machines last only one year. Later we will drop the simplifying assumption.

On January 1 the money wages earned and the money profits made during the previous year are in piles, too. Profits are understood broadly as all the money that firms make before they pay dividends to shareholders and interest to banks and bondholders, before they spend it to buy back some of their stock, etc.*

If the two output piles sell in full, the two money piles in full just purchase them. Wages and some of the profit purchase the consumption goods; the rest of the profit purchases the means of production. The money profit of the previous year exists in the January 1 output pile as means of production and items of capitalists' consumption, and the money wages of the previous year exist in the output pile as workers' consumption goods. We must trace the disruptive effects of accumulation in order to determine the reality and conditions of this balance.

In order to examine the consequences of innovative investments, we assume the workforce is a constant size.[88]

During the prosperity phase, the model must meet two conditions. First, there must be full employment in the capitalist sense. Employment is "full" (capital exploits as much labor as possible) if higher employment would trigger a rapid rise in wages, whether because workers bargain for increases or because capitalists outbid each other for workers in their eagerness to meet strong demand. Capitalist full employment is enough unemployment to keep wage increases from eating up profits. This condition is the best that capitalism achieves, except for rare moments. Economists try to hide the class dynamic

---

* This entity prior to the various forms of distributed profit is known as surplus value, but we will use a more common term, profits.

by calling it frictional unemployment, as though the only question is the time needed for a laid-off worker to find a new job. In fact, unemployment is a capitalist necessity.

Second, the money profit must be entirely spent on new means of production or capitalists' consumption. Workers will spend all their wages on consumption needs. We ignore workers' savings; they would not significantly affect the motion of the model. With this second condition, all the money on January 1 will exactly suffice to buy the piles of instruments of production and consumption goods.

The model is static or smoothly circular at this point. The object of study must be innovation within its structure.

❖

Some of the new means of production in the January 1 pile are disruptive. They replace instruments of an older design, rendering them obsolete. The capitalist, instead of buying the same equipment he used last year (which has worn out under temporary assumption), installs a new kind of machine. Accumulation is dynamic, changing the methods of making products and, even more unsettling, introducing new products produced by new methods. Old products made by new methods are cheaper. New products take demand away from old products, undercutting their profitable production because they can only be sold in smaller volume or at a lower price, or both.

When capital changes its instruments of production, only some of the workers find jobs operating the new instruments. Such is the case with the same product produced by new, cheaper methods; fewer workers are required to make the same number of output items. It might require more workers, more work hours, to make the new machines than the old ones, but capitalists buy them because savings on labor operating the new machine are greater than its extra cost. If a new machine is simply cheaper than the old one, but equally productive, again, fewer workers are needed to make it. A rarer case: a machine is less productive and requires more labor to operate, than the one it displaces, but it is vastly cheaper; here, too, the displacement of labor occurs where the machine is made.

Wholly new products attract buyers who shift their spending from other items. New products fulfill the function of old ones at lower cost. Indeed, they may be useful for a variety of functions, diminishing purchases of several old products. Novel products also arouse new needs that people rank higher than some existing needs.

In partial counterbalance, because buyers now satisfy some needs at lower cost, they can buy more of some existing products for other needs, products not affected by current technological changes. Whatever the mix, buyers can do more with their money. Of course, the shift of purchases from some things to others does not change the amount of money they spend.*

New products that displace old ones are introduced within the constraint of profit. Economists are fond of saying that the needs of people are limitless, suggesting that markets can grow endlessly. Under capitalism, everyone

---

* Some new products neither save cost nor displace spending on other categories of goods. An example is a simple change of fashion, perhaps the favored color of the year. We ignore this sort of "innovation."

but the very well-to-do must manage an economy of needs.

Needs largely derive from requirements for participation in the economy. We need food not simply to stay alive but because we must have enough energy to work and maintain the level of health that the job requires. We use transportation to get to work, shop for consumption items, and visit offices to transact business. Educational and information needs are shaped primarily by occupation – in childhood and youth, one's hoped-for occupation; during work years, one's current occupation. Most workers live their entire lives coping with unmet needs.

People's needs expand with the expansion of productive powers. As recently as 1990, access to the Internet was not a daily necessity. Twenty years later everyone needs a device to connect if she wants to find and keep a job, resolve a problem with a corporation or government agency, and shop intelligently. Lack of access to the Internet has become a new dimension of poverty for some. This is the fact even though trivial uses of the Internet consume the great majority of its bandwidth.

Some needs arise out of living under the pressures of exploitation and in the face of social obstacles to a fulfilling life. To salve the wounds, advertising and commercial mass culture sell things that offer cheap thrills (for example, games and movies soaked in violence), a bit of pride (a car that conveys a status niche with its sheet metal), emotional distraction (most mystery and romance novels), and the numbing of anxiety (drugs).

Official economics cannot discern the origin of needs because its practitioners exclude study of the rightful object of the field – the mode of production and its consequences.

❖

New instruments of production increase productiveness. After some of them absorb displaced workers, there remain more displaced workers and new instruments of production. They are available to produce more things, both new items in greater quantity than the amount that displaced old items, and existing items that people or capitals want in greater quantity. We say "or capitals" because the instruments might be intended to produce more means of production. Capital may increase the real investment portion of social product. This change is possible but not necessary. If the investment portion of social product remains unchanged, then consumer buying power remains unchanged, but it can buy more things because of increased productiveness. The actual situation can be a mix of the two expansions. While accumulation is vigorous, the remaining workers are hired to operate the remaining instruments of production. Capitalist full employment continues, and demand exists to buy the output.

Since the output price includes profit, capitalist expectations are fulfilled. In this sense – limited to the prosperity phase of accumulation – investment creates the demand for its output and generates the profits necessary to validate the investment.[89]

Output and demand balance, but only if the remaining equipment absorbs the labor of precisely the remaining displaced workers. This question depends on the technique of the instruments. How much labor does their operation require? A happy match of equipment and workers cannot be assumed, but real processes circle in to a balance. During the race to grow during prosperity, investment may absorb workers so quickly that instruments of production are left over after all displaced workers are reabsorbed. When attempted investment runs up against capitalist full employment, upward wage pressure pushes firms toward more capital-intensive methods. This is possible because a range of technical recipes for producing something are available. At one end, elaborate machines minimize the direct labor time per item of output. At the other end, the machinery is less elaborate and less costly but requires more direct labor time per item of output. The adoption of equipment that needs fewer workers continues until upward wage pressure relaxes.

Conversely, although less likely during prosperity, means of production that remain in the January 1 pile might not reabsorb all the remaining displaced workers. In this case, falling wages make adoption of the most elaborate capital-intensive methods uncompetitive, pushing toward the use of more labor-using methods.

The model shows us that accumulation can proceed under conditions of prosperity, namely, capitalist full employment and complete reinvestment of profit in means of production. During the year, firms get indications of where costs and demand are going. Some of the knowledge is foresight based on projections. Some of it comes from watching how new products sell (one's own, an innovation by a little guy, or in the worst case a new item from a major competitor). We may shorten the period of the model, too. From day to day, firms make adjustments in response to projections and results.* The model obviously simplifies economic reality; however, it traces realistic adjustments

---

* In effect, the model traces differential changes and their integration.

as capitals search for profit, choose what and how much to produce, and select from a range of technical methods of production.

❖

Capital accumulates in prosperity, period after period of the model. All is well – except for the contradiction that tears prosperity apart.

We drop the initial assumption that all instruments of production last exactly one year. There is a stock of capital value sunk into equipment that capitalists purchased one, two, three and many years ago. They must recover the outlay, for example by setting aside a certain amount from the sale of each item of output.

If the money is deposited in a depreciation fund, it is available to purchase replacement equipment. Ideally, the fund reaches that point at the moment when the equipment can no longer be used, but depreciation over a period of years brings the individual capitalist additional uncertainty. The equipment may become unusable before its cost has been recovered, because constant repair and maintenance are larger than was estimated, or because new kinds of machinery produce the output at much lower cost. Output from the old means can no longer be sold for a profit nor even cover marginal costs, mainly wages and raw materials. The shortfall is a loss of capital.

The opposite imbalance between depreciation and reality can occur, too. The capitalist may recover the investment, there has been little technical change, and the machinery still works fine. The situation is comfortable for an individual capital, although it is often a sign of monopoly complacency.

During prosperity there is profit, it is all realized in real goods, and capitalists do not consume it in full. Net investment is positive, and the stock of capital value increases from period to period.

Some of the new equipment is used to produce an amount of output that just captures the demand previously spent on the output of scrapped equipment. The value of the equipment may be more or less than the value recovered from the scrapped means of production during their operation (sitting in the depreciation fund). When the value is less, this is sometimes described as cheapening of constant capital. This fact should not confuse the overall accounting. The capital value in depreciation is reinvested, and so are the (unconsumed) profits of the year. If constant capital becomes cheaper during prosperity, capitalists buy more of it. Each period maintains and increases the total capital value.

Technology enables but does not drive the increase of capital in equipment. In the prosperity phase, capital reinvests all unconsumed profit because more gain beckons.

Capitalists invest when they judge that they can make a profit. Each capitalist is concerned only with the opportunities he finds. He ranks them by their rate of profit, the amount of profit in ratio to the money he must invest to get it. A capitalist's individual profit draws from the total profit available.

There is a general rate of profit, too: the total profit in ratio to the money invested, which in the model is carried in the stock of means of production. All the money invested in them is the total capital invested.

During the prosperity phase, the general rate of profit declines. The total capital swells; that is the denominator in the profit ratio. The numerator is the total profit of the period, which in the model is approximately constant. Hence the decline. The workforce is assumed constant, capitalist full employment of them is a condition of prosperity, and also during prosperity the division of output between the consumption that workers buy with their wages and the two parts of profit (investment goods and capitalist consumption) stays approximately the same.[90]

In this examination total output is measured at its value. Because productiveness increases, the value is spread over more things from one period to the next. (More of some things are produced, and new things take spending away from old things.) It is plausible that workers improve their material condition during prosperity by meeting more of their consumption needs even while the wage share of output remains constant. Needs are satisfied with real things, which benefit from increased productiveness.

During most of the prosperity phase, the fall of the general rate of profit is not a problem. For various reasons an accurate, current figure is not available. The individual capitalist does not care about the general rate of profit. If he gets an innovative product to market in time to capture demand for it, he makes a profit. If demand for his unchanged product is robust, he is happy.

Other capitalists find demand for their output slackening. Is the pace of decline at a rate they anticipated when they made the investment long ago? Capitalists have leeway in recognizing (in the accounting sense) destruction of capital value. During prosperity some output meets expanded demand for existent products produced without change of technique. Thus, machinery may continue to produce although it is not technically up to date. However, it still operates at a profit, and nothing compels the capitalist to write down his investment. The business continues; a decline in its rate of profit is not a disaster, although it is a warning about the future. How soon must the firm develop a new line of products?

Things are worse for some businesses. Every year some capitals lose money in the chaotic adjustments revealed in the market. If they borrowed to purchase equipment, they may not be able to make the loan payments. Until a certain point, individual capitalist losses do not threaten the prosperity phase.

At a level that cannot be deduced in advance, the rate of profit becomes so low that it derails accumulation. The effect is felt through various channels. For one, the projected return on individual investments is a range according to risk, the unpredictable effects that will arise in the future from the investments of competing capitals. As the range of projected returns shifts down, more contemplated investments become too risky for the likely return. Investments financed with debt prove to have been made on optimistic assumptions; because sales and profits drop, debt charges cannot be paid.

A falling rate of profit compels an end to prosperity accumulation. It falls while productiveness increases. A given workforce at capitalist full employment cannot operate more of the same kind of means of production year after year. Labor is more productive because of how it is done, which is intimately connected with the equipment it uses. The means of production change with innovation just like articles of consumption. Equipment is produced at lower unit cost with more productive labor.*

---

* Claims that increased productiveness of labor prevents the rate of profit from falling are mistaken. They revise on the sly the tally of value that capital has sunk into equipment, something

Their Analysis and Ours

Toward the end of prosperity when profits cannot find good investments in means of production, they may crowd into paper. A speculative bubble may unfold around real estate or in the most innovative industries, which issue stock offering a share of their prosperity. Of course, a growing sector should favor reinvestment of profit instead of dividends, which provides a perfect excuse for an exaggerated climb of share prices.

Financial booms do not create new profit, yet the appearance is the opposite. Hence the bigger the bubble, the harder the crash. You can let the air out of a balloon by opening your pinch on its neck or by blowing it up until it pops in your face. Secondary conditions determine whether prosperity passes into a bubble that bursts or whether it descends directly into a slump. Until the moment of truth, capitals may respond in a variety of ways to the tightening vise of a falling rate of profit.

Lack of demand does not cause the slump; it is a consequence of the problem with the rate of profit, hence with investment, hence total economic activity.

In the slump phase, workers lose their job or swallow wage cuts. Dashed hopes, anxiety, strained relationships, violence, and hunger spread. Some workers are caught in the downturn more than others, while bill collectors, food charities, and a few others do brisk business.

There is churn among capitalists, too. The slump forces destruction of invested capital. Perhaps only the money value disappears. For example, a firm goes bankrupt, buzzards swoop in to buy the assets on the cheap, and new owners restart the operation, able to produce

---

the capitalist himself cannot do. Unlike commentators, actual capitalists must recover their outlays before they have a profit.

with less money invested and also enforcing lower wages. Means of production are destroyed physically, too. A factory is blown apart and dismantled for the scrap value of the structural steel. Excess output of crops is plowed under. The denominator of the general rate of profit shrinks. Eventually, these actions clear the ground. Accumulation revives and a new phase of prosperity begins. The destruction visited on workers leaves lifelong scars.

❖

The contradiction that generates inevitable cycles of prosperity and slump reveals the arrogance of capital. Each year new profits are created. Their substance is surplus labor extracted from workers. Capital invests the profit; now it is capital, also expecting to live forever. The sum passes through several forms. Arriving as money profit, it becomes the capital value of means of production. The value passes into the output. When the output is sold, the capitalist invests the returned profit again along with the new surplus value. After some years the means of production wear out or become useless, but their value has been recovered and swelled by additional profit. The contradiction pits eternal capital value against the mortal life of material means of production. The crash or whatever ends a phase of prosperity delivers the shock that capitalized profits cannot expand forever.*

---

* Individual investments go bad all the time, like noise on a scratchy audio recording. The prudent business does not risk too much capital on any particular investment. Everyone, though, acts knowing more or less consciously that the total capital in the economy expands every year, except in the worst depth of slump.

Logic cannot resolve the contradiction of economic relationships. The capitalist put his money into the investment; of course he expects it back plus a reward. Most capitalists cannot see that their class seizure of a social function – allocating labor for new means of production – contains expectations of performing a miracle. The occasional capitalist who might understand what goes on will not agree to write off or give away his capital any more than the most ignorant person in his class.

Taking a look ahead, one sees how a rational society run by those who do the work may make investments and redistribute their labor without the presumption of eternal life for profit-yielding capital. Suppose firms operate to break even, not to make a profit. They finance new means of production with loans from public investment banks, similarly run to recover the principal, not yield interest. A firm is expected to pay back the loan during the useful life of the means. This accounts for the firm drawing on the labor embodied in them. When the firm completes repayment of the loan, the funds disappear, just like the machinery. There is no accumulation of dead capital value, no profit rate on swelling capital, hence no slump.*

Accumulation is the capitalist approach – through money, greed, and the struggle of capitals against each other – to the process of redistributing labor. All societies discard old means and work with new, sometimes improved ones. Before capitalism, the growth of productive

---

* Breakeven may be enforced on firms by levying a tax on all the work hours they employ; a social fund captures what was formerly private surplus value. For a rational method of allocating social labor to investments, including ways to deal with the inevitable failures and extraordinary successes, see this writer's *From Capitalism to Equality*, chapters nine and ten.

power was much slower. From the Renaissance, the pace quickened century after century and then decade after decade. Capitalism has its place. The struggle of capitals for profit introduced continual, deliberate innovation into history. The advance of productiveness into the scientific-technical phase prepares capitalism to be ushered out of history.

3.

The Third Contradiction
of Capitalist Accumulation

Capitalist relations of production exclude stable full employment in the common meaning of "full." This is the first fundamental contradiction of capitalism.

The prosperity phase of accumulation inevitably falls into slump. This is the second fundamental contradiction of capitalism. Still, a rising trend of industrial development and workers' struggles won a better life for many.

Relative mass prosperity ended around 1973 – a consequence of a third contradiction. The first two appeared early on; the third one emerges late in the life of the capitalist order.

Workers' real earnings keep going down, and recoveries from recessions take successively longer. Even Larry Summers, an ideological courtesan of financial capital, is upset. He gave a speech in November 2013 noting that the crash of 2008 had been repaired financially by 2010, but the percentage of people in the labor force had still not recovered. He recalled that he, the International Monetary

Fund, and the World Bank (in that order) projected Japan's real GDP twenty years out, yet actual Japanese GDP today is about half the projection. Summers publicly worried that secular stagnation had arrived.[91]

We must examine the rise of scientific-technical innovation in light of the accumulation model. The new mode of innovation wraps itself around the prosperity phase and squeezes it to death.

Accumulation is the capitalist process by which labor is redistributed in the course of changing what is produced. The redistribution has two parts: it expels workers from their current jobs, and it takes up workers in new work. Expulsion occurs in the cost-reducing aspect of accumulation. It includes both the reduced cost of making a basically unchanged product as well as the introduction of new products that meet consumers' needs at a lower cost than the products they displace. Scientific-technical innovation resembles earlier industrial innovation in this respect.

We saw that industrial capitalism could take up all the expelled workers in the prosperity phase of the accumulation cycle. Scientific-technical innovation gradually became a major force during the second half of the twentieth century. It created a corps of scientists, engineers, and technicians, as well as managers of their work, but this group remained a small portion of the workforce. On the other hand, new industries failed to hire large numbers of the displaced industrial workers.

For example, flexible manufacturing systems (FMSs) combine a whole line of workstations under central computer control. They were a new and highly advanced level of manufacturing automation in 1984. A federal government review found that FMSs were at an early prototype

stage. The researchers concluded, "Programmable automation producers especially are likely to employ relatively
few production personnel; their situation may signal future patterns among other firms and industries. Conse-
quently, there will be few opportunities for people
displaced from other manufacturing industries to move into jobs among producers of automated equipment and
systems."[92]

During the massive growth of the automobile and as-
sociated industries, output expanded by building new factories that hired large numbers of workers. Although the
process of mechanizing production was continuous from
the beginning, it began to reduce employment by significant amounts late in the arc of the industry. As our scientific-technical powers develop, mass employment hardly
gets underway. From the start, machines, robots and
chemical vats attended by few workers perform more steps
of production.

Further innovation carries a science-based industry
to its next generation, the equipment changes, but the
number of workers required to produce vastly more output
does not increase or barely increases. The classic example
is a new generation of semiconductors. The new fabrication equipment produces chips twice as dense as the previous generation, and they run faster. The research and
design staff engineers the new chips. Technical and craft
workers make the machines. Production of transistors and
chips doubles. The scientists, engineers, technicians, and
some industrial and clerical staff move to the next generation of innovation. The specialties of the staff change
somewhat; the number of people changes little.

A cumulative feature of scientific-technical innovation
touches a more profound reason for the net shrinkage of

routinized labor. This is the "limit to what human muscle and nerve can do when they are used repetitively and with limited education. Although we can work longer and more intensely than people a century ago, although we are taller (and lately, fatter), we are basically the same physiological beings we have been for thousands of years. There is also a limit to mental speedup, the multitasking demanded of workers today. Every year machines have less need for the assisting eyes, ears, and hands of industrial labor. Humans seem unable to keep up because of their physiological limits, but the limits apply only because capitalism insists that most work must be industrial labor and most workers must be human machines. It is no surprise that machines based on advancing science finally push them aside."[93]

Transistors disappear from sight, at first from bare vision then from squints through a microscope. Fingers can no longer insert wires at the tiny scale of semiconductor junctions. The hand, eye, and brain are ousted from production.

The effects are progressive over time. New products enable new processes that take over a still wider portion of the capabilities of semiskilled and skilled labor.

❖

What is the net effect of scientific-technical methods of production on the economic position of standard labor? We can trace how accumulation displaces and takes up workers in the model of the prosperity phase.

Innovative investment displaces old equipment and the workers employed at them. Only some of them are taken up in producing for the same demand that the discontinued items met. This is the initial displacing output of new items.

An additional quantity of new items is produced, too. Even if personal computers did nothing but replace typewriters, some people would buy them who had never purchased a typewriter in order to produce neat documents. The additional output grabs purchasing power that had been spent on unrelated things serving unrelated purposes; buyers prefer to spend their money on the new thing.

Actually, personal computers appealed to a wider range of uses than the main purpose of typewriters, writing neat documents. For example, you can play computer games that you may enjoy more than a board game. You can do bookkeeping that used to be done with mechanical calculators, pencils and ledger forms. More radically, new products may arouse new wants and satisfy new needs.

The potential expansion of output that sustains prosperity and hires displaced workers is of three categories: one, more of the new products beyond their initial displacing output, which we have just discussed; two, more existing items produced in new ways with less labor; and three, more existing items produced in unchanged ways.

The second category, expanded output of existing products produced in more productive ways, is an amalgam of the first and third categories. The lower cost attracts more demand, but since the product itself is not new, it upsets the distribution of demand among all products less than the first category. Production for expanded demand takes up workers, but the enlarged volume of output is produced in a more productive way, hence taking up standard labor with less vigor than the third category.

The third category, increased output of existing items produced in unchanged ways, amounts to a rearguard action as far as taking up standard labor. In the decades of transition from industrial to scientific-technical innovation, the roster of industrial products shrinks, counting for less and less of the total output value. Period after period in the model (a year, for example), more of the existing products are the result of previous rounds of scientific-technical innovation. Demand for them might increase, but there is little need for routinized labor in their production.

For example, in the year 2000 during the so-called dot-com boom based on growth of the consumer Internet, prosperity might lead to increased purchases of microwave ovens, too. Let's get a second microwave for the home theater room! Microwave ovens are an old science-based product; they had reached three out of five homes by 1976. They displaced stoves in much of home food preparation, and they are made with less industrial labor than stoves. The key part, the magnetron that generates the microwaves, is made on completely automated production lines.[94]

When the basis of accumulation developed from industrial innovation to scientific-technical innovation over the latter half of the twentieth century, it broke up the balances and adjustments that supported phases of capitalist prosperity. The march of accumulation no longer rotates standard labor out of shrinking industries into expanding new ones. Scientific-technical innovation expels standard labor, and the take-up of workers for routinized labor falters. Looking over the three categories of such take-up, the first category expands output mostly by automated methods; the third category slowly shrinks into nothingness starting from the middle of the twentieth century; and the second category is a combination of the other two. A cadre of innovation employees remains a small portion of the workforce while accumulation shrinks mass employment sectors of production.

By weaving the change into the model of accumulation, watching how it emerges from period to period, we recognize that the singular historic development is distinct from recurring cycles of accumulation. Cycles result from a fall in the rate of profit built into accumulation; the change from industrial to scientific-technical innovation is long-term and relentless in one direction. Cycles express a contradiction in the ordinary functioning of industrial capitalism. The sputtering economy since 1973 manifests an emergent contradiction signaling the end of capitalism.

The consequence is unrelieved downward pressure on the wages of standard labor. Falling real wages raise the bar for automation, but the effect is only one of delay. Scientific-technical innovation keeps reducing the cost of equipment that replaces standard labor. At first, a robot is economically viable in a few specialized uses. Then its cost of production falls, and so does the wage that would stave off replacement.

Norbert Wiener observed that no team of ditch diggers with hand shovels could compete with a steam shovel. A competitive wage would not buy them enough food and warmth to stay alive. Their way out was factory jobs, and the basic education necessary for a boy to become a factory hand instead of a ditch digger was available. We shall see, after examining trends in investment in means of production, that capitalism cannot allow standard labor to become qualified labor.

❖

The principal avenue for introducing technological change is investment in equipment. A snapshot of the categories of real investment, decade to decade from 1950 to 2000, illustrates the developments traced so far. (See Table 3 at end.) In 1950 industrial equipment, primarily used in manufacturing, comprised 54 percent of all real investment in equipment and software. The investment increased slightly to 56 percent in 1960, which is within the range of short-term business fluctuations. We saw earlier that manufacturing was the site of considerable scientific-technical innovation, as shown by its employment pattern, the technology content of the faster-growing industries, and many examples of how manufacturing automated. Although sensors and logic were built into new machines, we presume that government statistics still counted the investment as industrial equipment.

Statistical categories lag behind real change. At this time the category of information processing equipment recorded investment in standalone mainframe computers, for example. Its rapid growth was apparent, although we do not have a breakdown here of industrial applications versus use by banks to process checks, utilities to bill customers, and other business activities.

Industrial equipment as a portion of all equipment and software investment was 50 percent of the total in 1980. The drop in industrial machinery as a portion of investment accelerated during the 1980s, falling to 42 percent in 1990. All this happened before the export of jobs to China and Eastern Europe took off in the 1990s. By 1990, investment purchases of computer equipment and software exceeded investment in industrial equipment.*

The spread of scientific-technical innovation undermined net investment. Total or gross real investment consists of two parts: new equipment and facilities that replace old equipment, and additional new means.† In conventional terms, gross investment equals depreciation plus net investment.

Measurement of depreciation is difficult, so we read the data only for the most prominent changes. The chart is calculated on depreciation; as it grows, net investment shrinks.[95] The fitted trend line shows what happened through the ups and downs of accumulation cycles: the ratio of net investment to gross investment shrank from 1950 to 2011.

---

* Transportation equipment went to both rail and air transport in the 1950s, then more to air. "Other equipment" is spread broadly over furniture and fixtures, and machinery used in agriculture, construction, mining, oil drilling, and service industries.

† The division is measured by the value of the means, in the sense of the labor theory of value. We disregard the problems of capitalist foresight, assuming that all means of production return the value invested in them just as they go out of service.

Depreciation / gross investment,
private nonresidential assets

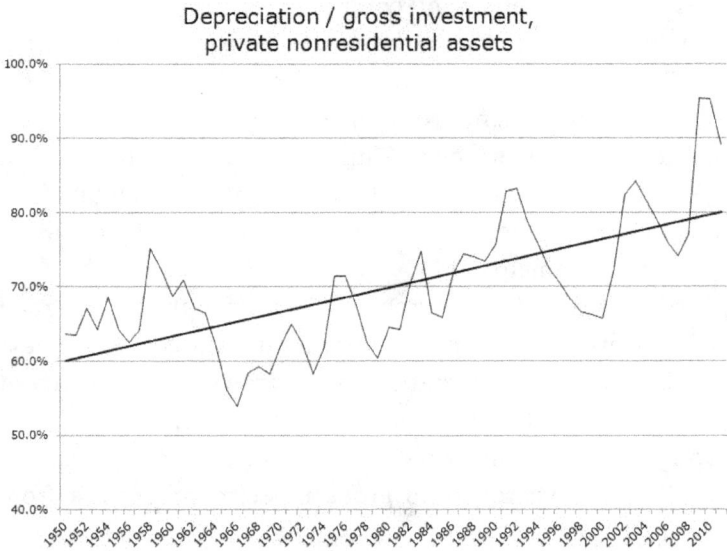

The equipment, processes, and software used in production based on scientific-technical innovation have a shorter economic life than was typical of industrial equipment. Already in 1987 the U.S. Bureau of Economic Analysis concluded "that the average service life of computers is eight years, nearly the shortest of any type of capital. Metal-working equipment, for example, lasts 16 years, railroad equipment 28 years..."[96]

A later development is also apparent from Table 3. The combined investment in information processing equipment and software displays a sign of maturity around 2000. Their share had grown substantially in every prior decade. From 2000 to 2010, it grew only three percentage points, while the share of industrial equipment grew two percentage points.

The Third Contradiction of Capitalist Accumulation

❖

When scientists and engineers can advance a field routinely, innovation in an industry continues for several decades. Typically in this situation, the life of investments is short. The reason is not purely technical. An era of continual innovation alters the capitalist struggle to capture profits. The most famous statement of the phenomenon is called Moore's Law, although its discoverer did not state the necessity that makes it a law. In 1965 Gordon E. Moore, an engineer-capitalist who co-founded Intel Corporation three years later, observed that the density of transistors on a given area of semiconductor silicon doubles every two years. Despite continual worries that a physical limit of density would be reached and put a ceiling on the trend, it has prevailed for more than 55 years.

In the industrial era, by contrast, a new technological process developed turbulently for several years. Improvement upon improvement was devised quickly and at little expense, but soon further advance would require major research. Then innovation subsided. It was too costly, considering the risk of finding no solution for a long time, or of producing with a technique that competitors might implement almost as easily as the research-funding capital. Instead, surviving capitals from the brief tempestuous phase comfortably used their equipment for many years, even decades, with small modifications at best.

While visiting England in 1872, Andrew Carnegie toured the steel mill of Henry Bessemer. His furnaces implemented the first workable process of mass-producing steel from molten iron. Carnegie, already a wealthy businessman, built a large mill in Braddock, Pennsylvania using the Bessemer process. From its startup in 1875

Carnegie funded managers' continual recommendations to replace and add equipment. A recent biography quotes from a July 1877 letter that a manager of Carnegie's main steelworks wrote. During a shutdown for repairs, he "put in some additional machinery." It worked admirably and "gives us complete control of rail from rolls to hot bed, and also allows us to dispense with services of two men and two boys, saving us at least $100 on wages, and as the machine did not cost of $100 you will see that it is a very good investment."[97]

Carnegie dallied with the open hearth furnace, too. Commercial experiment began as early as 1884 in England,[98] but a fully equipped steel firm like Carnegie's could not fund sustained development to improve it. In 1896, production by open hearth furnaces was still less than 15 percent of steel output.[99] The furious pace of innovation had drifted to a halt. Five years before J.P. Morgan bought out Carnegie and merged producers into the U.S. Steel monopoly in 1901, Carnegie's early enthusiasm for capital outlays had cooled. He said, "Nothing requires more conservatism than the manufacture of steel."[100] U.S. Steel was notoriously stodgy about innovation for half a century.

Why not operate a semiconductor fabrication plant for decades like a steel mill? The amortization of the plant would make the rectangles of printed silicon incredibly cheap. The problem for capital is that today when a branch of science reaches a certain level, ongoing research yields significant productive advances year after year in the exponential manner of Moore's Law. The scientists and engineers open a field like quantum electronics or DNA manipulation. It is visible but not well understood; investment is too risky. At a takeoff moment it becomes routinely exploitable by capitalist innovation for decades.*

The consequence is a pattern of short "generations" of technology. Soon after one fab process goes into production, capital can build a more advanced fab that produces chips containing twice as many transistors per square millimeter. The old chips become obsolete, and with them the old equipment. Every capital must recover its investment and yield a profit quickly, before the next innovative step arrives. The innovation may be financed and carried out by a company that understands the process, or one company may seize a market from another company.[101] A self-described "telephone company nerd" writing at his desk in AT&T Labs in 1997 described the cannibalism of the insightful corporation: "Intel does it – having been the first to articulate Moore's Law, it now drives it with a new, more powerful chip every 18 months or so, long before the old chip is obsolete – it realizes that if it stops, there are other chip makers that would be glad to take leadership of that market."[102]

From 1950 real investment was increasingly based on "high tech" innovation. Products became outmoded and their means of production were scrapped more quickly.

---

* It has been apparent for at least twenty years that nuclear transformations occur within suitable materials in "tabletop" apparatus at ordinary external temperatures and pressures, unlike attempts to mimic the fusion that occurs within the sun. The media call it cold fusion, but that is a misnomer for a variety of nuclear reactions. A vast new source of power and the capability of transforming one element into another await. So far, though, neither private capital nor their governments see a low-risk, high-profit opportunity. They are not willing to put large sums into developing the science, scientists, and engineers.

Depreciation funds went into innovative replacements, embodying much of the investment aiming for individual profit.

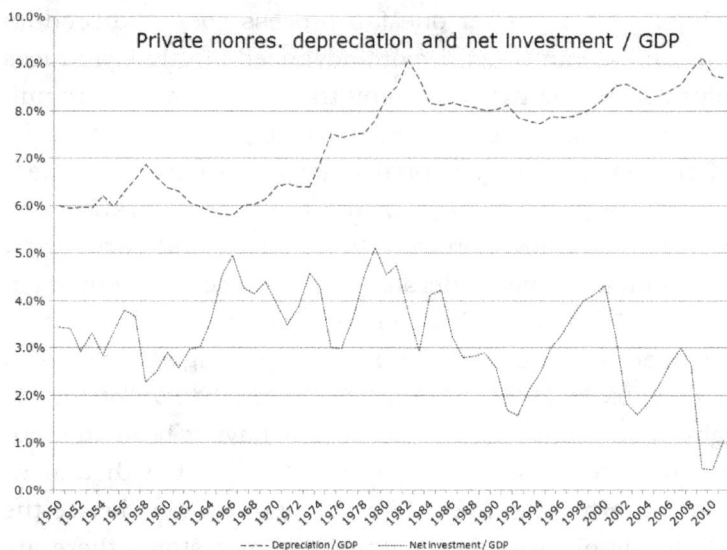

Private nonres. depreciation and net Investment / GDP

Across the economy as a whole, the average period for depreciating investments became shorter. We saw that from 1950 to 2011 depreciation grew as a percentage of gross investment while net investment fell. The data display two phases within the six decades. We track depreciation and net investment as a percentage of all capitalist output, taking GDP as a rough stand-in for output. There is a dividing point around 1979. Before then, net investment held steady or rose slightly, averaged over cycles, while depreciation as a percentage of GDP rose steadily from a low point in 1965. After 1979, net investment began a long decline in relation to output, again averaging over cycles, while depreciation remained level.[103]

The Third Contradiction of Capitalist Accumulation

❖

A few details of wages and other compensation fill out the picture of real wages since 1973. Especially stark is the failure of job and wage revival from the 2008 recession. Two causes undermine recovery. One, structural problems in the economy may be partially masked during normal times, but they emerge rapidly when a slump arrives. Another reason is that the long, gradual absorption of women into the workforce finished around 2000. Before then, workforce trends were a result of severely worse terms for men partially offset by gains for women. Since 2000, men and women workers share common negative trends.

The National Employment Law Project sorted 366 detailed occupations into three layers: low-wage, mid-wage, and higher-wage. How did jobs shift from the onset of the recession in the first quarter of 2008 to the first quarter of 2010, and then during anemic recovery from 2010 to 2012?

"Lower-wage occupations [like retail sales and food preparation] constituted 21 percent of recession job losses, but fully 58 percent of recovery growth. Mid-wage occupations constituted 60 percent of recession job losses, but only 22 percent of recovery growth. Higher-wage occupations constituted 19 percent of recession job losses, and 20 percent of recovery growth."[104]

The study also went back eleven years and found, "Since the first quarter of 2001, employment has grown by 8.7 percent in lower-wage occupations and by 6.6 percent in higher-wage occupations. By contrast, employment in mid-wage occupations has declined by 7.3 percent since the first quarter of 2001." In addition, the real pay in low-

and mid-wage occupations fell, while it rose in higher-wage occupations.[105]

Inequality became a fashionable topic in 2013. Most statistics emphasize the exorbitant wealth and income of the "one percent" that Occupy protests made famous two years earlier. The outlandish polarization goes right up to one family in ten thousand, the one percent of the one percent. For the working class a whole, a useful measure is how much of gross domestic income (GDI) goes to employee compensation. (See figure.)[106] Wages and salaries peaked at 53.5 percent of GDI in 1970, then fell in 26 of the next 41 years to 44.2 percent in 2011.

Total compensation supplied fodder for controversy over whether things are really so bad. The wage and salary figure does not include benefits paid by the employer. These are primarily health plans, retirement accounts and, to a lesser extent, the employer share of payroll taxes for the public equivalents, Medicare and Social Security. This supplemental compensation grew as a percentage of GDI until about 1980, then stabilized. There is a difficulty, however, in adding supplemental compensation to current wage income. Health care has grown to be the major supplemental component, and the inflation of health care costs runs well above the general inflation rate. The money that employers undeniably pay out overstates what workers receive when it is treated the same as dollars of the basic wage. The alleged trend over the years is skewed by the fact that workers buy bread, clothes, and so on out of shrinking real wages, while they are lucky to maintain the same health coverage.

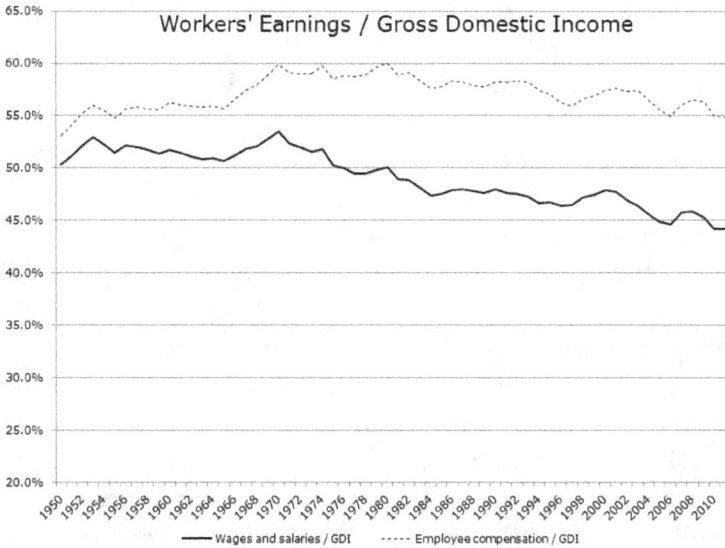

Workers' Earnings / Gross Domestic Income

Wages and salaries / GDI   Employee compensation / GDI

Workers know what is going on: they use their limited bargaining power simply to keep health coverage, foregoing wage increases. The statistics agree. We can calculate the correlation between wages and supplemental compensation, taking both as percentages of GDI. There was little connection between them from 1950 to 1973; their correlation coefficient was a weakly positive 0.21. However, from 1974 to 2011 the correlation was a strongly negative -0.83.[107] This result is consistent with trading off a wage hike, or accepting a reduction, in order to keep the same health plan.[108]

Personal income may be viewed from a different angle. It includes government transfer payments to workers, retired workers, the unemployed, and poor people outside the workforce. These are Social Security, Medicare and Medicaid, food stamp and welfare benefits, unemployment insurance, veterans benefits and other programs. They amounted to 15 percent of GDI in 2011, including a sub-stantial rise with the onset of the great recession of 2008.[109] Much of the long term growth of government pay-ments was in Medicare and Medicaid.

Such payments are the occasion for another fashion-able attempt at refuting the shrinking share of labor in na-tional income. It would be an error simply to add this money to labor earnings. Workers pay a good chunk of the taxes that finance the benefits. In addition, many recipi-ents are retired workers; it would be double counting to tally employer contributions when they worked and then the benefit received when they are in retirement.

However, let us forget for a moment about class rela-tions of employment and look instead at household ine-quality before and after government collects taxes and disburses transfer payments. It would be scandalous if the effect were to heighten inequality, but how much does government "for the people" soften inequality? According to the Congressional Budget Office, in 2010 the lowest-income fifth of households got 2.3 percent of income be-fore government action but 9.3 percent after taxes and transfers. They are delivered from immediate starvation to a condition of limping along. We must remember, too, that many the people in this stratum work, full time or part time, steady hours or on call. However, their jobs pay so little that they qualify for food stamps, Medicaid, and oth-er transfer programs. At the other end, the top fifth (a broad group that dilutes the stratospheric incomes of the top one-tenth of one percent) were left with "only" 47 per-cent of all the income instead of what would be 58 percent without government action.[110]

The Third Contradiction of Capitalist Accumulation

❖

Our investigation of capitalist accumulation assumed a strict wall between standard labor and nascent non-routinized labor. It is an element of the model that explains why prosperity erodes. What might break through this barrier? We briefly survey the development of education (the American solution, in words at least, for everything from inequality to obesity), and then we examine what capital does about non-routinized labor in health care and education.

With change in the techniques of production, the education of each new generation must develop, too. Setting aside tutelage within the ruling classes, we see changes in the education of those who do the work. In agrarian societies, peasants raised their children on the farm and in the household. Mother and father and other adults taught farming, textile crafts, and carpentry to the children in the course of the labor itself. Factory workers have a narrower range of skills, but soon it became necessary that they have the three R's – reading, writing, and 'rithmetic. People need them on the job, to be consumers, and simply to get around by reading signs. In addition, when labor markets became citywide, regional and national, working people required practical knowledge of how to find a job and go where it might be obtained.

To prepare workers for an industrial economy, mass elementary schooling arose in the latter half of the nineteenth century, extending to secondary education by the middle of the twentieth century. In 1950, 96 percent of children age 7 to 13 were enrolled in school, and 70 percent of eighteen- to twenty-year olds had completed at least a year of high school.[111] Despite the needs of an

113

economy that capital runs, the working class's hunger to give its children literacy and culture was a greater impetus for mass education. Fortunately for capital, it proved to be remarkably cheap. Expenditures in 1950 for elementary and secondary education, public and private, were less than one-fourth as much as private nonresidential investment. The portion of surplus devoted to mass education posed no threat to the accumulation of capital.[112]

When it comes to qualifying workers as scientific and technical personnel, the situation is different. We saw earlier that the personnel in research and development occupations remain a minority of the workforce. Despite the expansion of college enrollment and community colleges after World War Two, the percentage of people age 25 to 34 with a year or more of college climbed to just under 24 percent in 1977 then stagnated at that level until 1994, when the urgency of education became unavoidable and the drive to go to college resumed, but at a slower pace. In 2010 those with a year or more of college were 33 percent of the age group. That is a healthy portion, although the important dividing line for earnings is the four-year college degree. It is likely that a majority of the workforce will not be college graduates for a long time. Furthermore, in 2010 almost half of college graduates were in occupations that do not require a college degree.[113]

Capitalist accumulation turned to scientific-technical innovation out of necessity, not desire. New stages of productive power affect the composition of the workforce, but always within the confines of the fact that the worker's capacity to labor is a commodity. More precisely, labor powers are tiers of commodities graded according to skill and qualification. The price of an engineer is greater than the price of a factory operative. The difference is at least the cost of making such a worker in youth, plus the cost of maintaining qualifications during his career. In fact, though, earnings in the occupations requiring the most preparation are much greater than cost explains. It takes more resources to produce an engineer than a routine industrial, office, or store worker. Many families do not have the necessary sum; those who do are able to command a premium salary. Such, at least, was the mechanism in the heyday of the growth of professional occupations.

Government grants, scholarships and other aid in those days enabled some people to become highly qualified workers who otherwise could not afford it. Such aid can partially equalize the resources required to obtain higher levels of education. There is not much substance to the American myth of equal opportunity if everything depends on how rich your parents are. However, the wealthy as a class also have the time and concern to make sure in politics that outright scholarships and grants are confined to a small stratum of youth.

These youth are often said to have the most merit, a mysterious quality that promises a big payoff for society if we choose meritorious people to receive education and high-level jobs. There has never been a reverse application of the idea of merit: if the child of a well-to-do family is not really a good candidate for higher education, he is barred from taking a college slot. It should go to someone of greater merit. No one wants such a rigorous meritocracy, but the mere thought of it reveals the deep problems of selecting for merit in a society of unequal wealth.

❖

Although innovation requires qualified personnel, jobs for them remain a small portion of total employment. Capital looks for ways to reduce the amount of highly qualified labor needed for a production process. Where production is done with skill, judgment and individual attention, capital substitutes routinized production performed by machines and ordinary industrial labor. In addition to the hard cost comparison, capital by instinct attacks skilled work that gives the worker responsibility to evaluate whether a result is satisfactory.

As examples of the antagonism to engaged labor, two large, growing, and contentious fields are worth a look: health care and education. The front-line occupation of class struggle in health care is the registered nurse (RN). The RN has at least two years of college training, which prepares her for intense formal and on-the-job apprenticeship. When you are in the hospital, your life is in the RN's hands. She is alert for signs of crisis in your body; she initiates the action that can save you. After a few hours around you, she has a picture of your strengths and vulnerabilities, how several conditions in your physiology interact, and your response to medications. She is a professional both by law and in the substance of the term.

Hospital managers regard RNs as an obstacle to reducing the cost of care per patient. Information technology (IT) comes to the managers' rescue with a pair of interventions. First, the RN is told to document the condition of the patient at a computer. Next, she is told to follow scripts from the computer that specify the treatment of the patient. The RN is supposed to plug herself into a circuit in which she subordinates her work to the processing of

116

data. Before IT arrived, she discussed each patient with the RNs who treated him before and after her shift. Directions for treatment came from a human being, the physician. The RN could point out relevant facts to him. Some doctors listen, and some notoriously do not.

The computer system never listens. At every juncture the patient is reduced to data. When the RN documents his pulse, skin tone, color of the lips, range of motion of a limb, and so on at a computer, she clicks choices from menus. Important comments are not allowed, or require extra effort to reach a note field that the software ignores. "Expert" programs zip from the menu entries to a specified course of treatment. A physician who reviews and approves the results of the program is under menu constraints, too. Does he take the time to see whether the RN made "unstructured" comments? If he goes against the program and then the patient turns for the worse, he bears responsibility for transgressing the program.

The payoff for the hospital is similar to the time and motion studies that Frederick Winslow Taylor's stopwatch men did more than a hundred years ago. Chart the activity of a man who shovels coal into a furnace; time each motion with a stopwatch; decide the one best way to do it; tell the man exactly how to do the job. Computerized patient records and expert systems do the same thing to the RN. Now that the hospital knows how much time every activity takes, it can assign more patients to each nurse. It reassigns some of her work to nonprofessional staff; they are not observers with seasoned judgment like an RN, but they are paid less. An expert system, fewer RNs, physicians told to spend less time per patient – this is the profit formula in the hospital industry.

Who designs the expert system that matches menu choices to recipes of treatment? Small circles of unaccountable persons write and review the programs. Hospitals and insurance companies buy them to reduce costs.

What disappears is care for the individual patient by RNs who know he is an actual person. The RN might agree with the program that he is likely to react in a certain way. But he might not, and if so, his care should take a different path *now*.

At its best expert software juggles probabilities drawn from research studies. No matter how well they do the job, it remains statistical. The basic fallacy in an expert system is the leap from statistics to the individual patient. A valid probability tells you that something will happen in, for example, 95 out of 100 cases. No one knows in advance which five cases are the exceptions. The RN's judgment, built up from reflection on experience, offers insight that the statistics do not. That judgment is gone. With bitter statistical certainty, we can say that individual patients die under treatment by modern, cost-saving information systems in hospitals.

The cold-hearted retort is that overall results are better. They might indeed improve over a period of time during which needless malady and death occur. That is small consolation to the individual who would have been saved except that an RN was not allowed to work as a professional.

We heard for decades how statins were the magic bullet against bad forms of cholesterol and hence heart attacks. Then more accurate research found that the link between cholesterol and heart trouble is not so simple. In the meantime statins caused all sorts of side effects. The large-scale studies evolved on their own slow path. When you take statins, you are advised not to eat grapefruit. Perhaps grapefruit do some people as much good for the cardiovascular system as statins. How many health care professionals treated individual patients, observed side effects, noticed that some kinds of patients were more susceptible to them, and wondered whether blanket prescription of statins was such a great thing? We do not know. Pharmaceutical companies guide the large-scale research, directly and through cozy ties with the decision-makers who fund research. They did not have, or had to set aside, deep discussions with front-line practitioners.

Information technology could be put to human use. Then it would help hospital staff *combine* their professional attention to each individual patient with research findings. They would exercise judgment, not follow computer programs with little time for reflection on the patient who lies in front of the RN and the physician. Information technology could be a tool for people who do what machines cannot. Instead, menu-driven patient records and expert systems reduce the RN and the physician to gears in a networked machine dedicated to cutting cost.

Large-scale medical research is a great thing. No one advocates a return to the physician in his office who educated himself fitfully after medical school, treating each patient as much with a comforting manner as with medical skill. The National Nurses United trade union called on the Food and Drug Administration to help make electronic patient records and so-called expert systems safe by requiring:

• Extensive government research and testing.

• Regulating health IT systems as medical devices at the highest level of oversight, such as is applied before replacement heart valves are approved.

• Protection for RNs and other health professionals to assure they have the freedom to override the diagnosis, prognosis, or treatment recommendations of the devices.

• Pre-testing of the devices, before they are used by a provider, and post-implementation and mandatory reporting of adverse events and near misses.

• Improved transparency, including the use of open source computer codes accessible and available on a public website.[114]

These requirements, especially the third and fifth items on the list, illuminate the clash between actual health care and the capitalist business of health care.

❖

Like registered nurses in health care, classroom teachers are the obstacle to those who want to slash to cost of universal primary and secondary education. Teaching is an art learned partly in college courses but mostly through motivated experience in the classroom, help from experienced colleagues, and the occasional professional workshop. Teachers acquire insight about the two dozen children entrusted to them and judgment about methods likely to help each individual child. A teacher "measures" her success with a child during the school year when she observes his ways of thought, his knowledge, emotional profile, and character. A significant advance for one child is not the same as for another. Parents see the progress, too. Tests, essays, and presentations to the class are part of such evaluation. The goal of raising the average score of a class 7.38 percent would have been laughable – until capital made it serious.

The Third Contradiction of Capitalist Accumulation

Capital has swung several bludgeons in an effort to destroy real teaching and reduce costs. We will not dwell on the vicious slander of teachers as a group. One instrument for destroying education is the charter school. Public funds are diverted to private groups, whether openly for-profit or allegedly nonprofit (yet leasing facilities, contracting operations, and purchasing supplies from favored companies). They are an end run around the teachers' union, which is confronted with the task of organizing anew a business entity that is legally separate from the school district.

Charter schools are not part of the community. They answer to local parents even less than the district does. Their relation to parents is the typical relation of a corporation to customers. They promote themselves around the entire city with boasts about test scores and perhaps the percentage of graduates who start college. In order to compete in this manner, the charter school nudges out students who do not score well on tests. Especially when a charter school targets a market of low-income families, it cuts costs by drilling children for tests and eliminating "frill" classes and activities.

Charter schools are still at the fringes of public education. They enrolled just under five percent of public school students in 2012, although the push is on to raise the percentage rapidly. One problem is their poor results. "The only major national evaluation of charter schools was carried out by Stanford economist Margaret Raymond and funded by pro-charter foundations. Her group found that compared to regular public schools, 17% of charters got higher test scores, 46% had gains that were no different than their public counterparts, and 37% were significantly worse."[115]

The Hollow Colossus

The main hammer against primary and secondary education is standardized tests that federal law imposes. Frequent tests are required. Administrators present the scores as measures of how effective teachers are. Overwhelmed by the burden of preparing for the next test, the teacher is unable to observe the individual child carefully, figure out his strong points and handicaps, consult colleagues and literature, and judge what to try next. Instead, the teacher must jam the narrow knowledge and routines of answering test problems onto the class. Her challenge is to make it clear to the students that they must get with the program.

Obviously, tests narrow the child's educational experience. A whole range of activities that can awaken talents and arouse cultural desires in children are excluded: seeing cause and effect by tinkering with radios as well as digital electronic circuits; cooperating in a musical performance; appreciating materials and the skills of working on them by shaping wood with simple tools; showing people how you see an object by depicting it on paper or in clay; exploring the paradoxical mix of feeling and calculated presentation by acting in a play. These activities – typical for humans, unknown to animals, and somehow not the same when a machine does them – are inefficient uses of time to improve a child's test scores. Away with them!

Teaching to the test deskills teaching. It is no surprise that what follows the imposition of a regime of tests, tests, tests is a Common Core curriculum and recipes for presenting it to the class. The curriculum mandates, for example, that fiction read by the child and read to the class by the teacher shall not exceed a specified percentage of all reading.

The battle is engaged. Teachers collectively can fight for real education in alliance with parents, or they can give up one by one. The capitalist vision is education transformed into a machine. Capital seeks to dissolve the skilled body of teachers into a mass of employees, beaten into taking orders from ambitious teacher-managers. The criterion is, how many children get a given score with the least input of teaching time at the lowest possible cost?

Wherever large numbers of skilled, autonomous workers like registered nurses and teachers work, capitalist forces mobilize to take skill and judgment out of their craft and profession, shift tasks to lower-paid workers, and substitute machines. These forces are expressed in part when individual capitals hunt for profitable investments. Deborah Quazzo, founder and managing partner of GSV Advisors, an investment firm specializing in education, said, "There's a lot of enthusiasm around trying to find innovative ways to bring greater access, lower costs ... to drive better learning efficacy." Private businesses were put off by "bureaucracy" and regulation, but Quazzo told an industry reporter that "several factors have changed the opportunity landscape for investors, including policy changes at the federal and local levels (such as Race to the Top and No Child Left Behind)."[116]

For-profit capitals already in the field are, however, only a small part of the general capitalist drive against education. Most schools may well remain public in name for a long time. One front of the capitalist offensive is about hollowing out public education. Bill Gates does not want to wait for complete, overt privatization before Microsoft can sell roomfuls of digital dreck to school districts as well as install networked surveillance of every child, making her a target for individualized marketing.

Gates is after big cuts in public spending on education. In a speech to the trade association of "public" charter schools, he whined, "Over the last 30 years society has invested substantially more in schools. There's been an increase in the average salary..."[117] Yes, Gates led off with a complaint about those women teachers who used to accept pitiful wages but now expect to be paid as much as the administrative assistants at Microsoft!

Does Gates see that most people will have junk jobs in "modern" capitalism? That would motivate him to push for dismantling the educational system that was built when industry employed masses in factories at the heart of accumulation. Gates may sense that the class war in education is contention over our economic future. Shall most people be ground down while a narrow elite destroys society in its scramble for riches? Or shall we terminate the accumulation of capital? Shall we have an economy of no rich and no poor in which people do work that meets the individual and public needs of all?

Innovations could provide nurses and teachers tools that they use as needed for human work. Capital, not a technological imperative, allows no room for such things. It introduces machines that chop their work into bits and pieces. Instead of a society of educated, far-seeing, and healthy people, we get one-dimensional test scores and bogus health indexes.

❖

Whatever the occupation, it struggles sooner or later against the depredations of capital accumulation.

However, registered nurses and K-12 teachers were somewhat unusual occupations under industrial capitalism. The technology that routinized them, a broad complex of information technologies, was developed late in the industrial era, and until the third quarter of the twentieth century, substandard pay for women kept costs down. Both health care and public education were relatively insulated from the drive to reduce costs in comparison with manufacturing, general clerical work, and other fields.

Public education was a matter of concern and pride to communities. The idea that it had to be narrowed to a few test scores in order to make it affordable did not arise. Rather, public schools were pressed to offer arts and to add special programs for children with distinct needs.

Health care, an industry that enjoyed strong demand for much of the twentieth century, was structurally capable of raising prices more rapidly than general inflation. Employers who provided health coverage depended on health insurance corporations to administer their program. The insurers, to the degree that their profits were a percentage on top of the prices that hospitals, physicians, and other providers charged, were not strongly motivated to restrain costs. When insurers did bargain aggressively, hospitals merged to form countervailing oligopolies in local markets.[118] The major government health insurance program, Medicare for people 65 and over, has made weak attempts to restrain price rises, usually by issuing lists of what it will pay for each detailed treatment and procedure. In response, hospitals and physicians have staffs who play a game of "upcoding" treatments. Operations are done for revenue even when there is no medical necessity for them.

The situation began to change in the 1990s; national health care expenditures passed ten percent of gross domestic product. By 2009 health care expenditures were almost fifteen percent of GDP.[119] The push has been on to cheap and deny care, while hospitals, health insurance corporations, drug firms, and the other capitalists feeding at the trough maintain their prosperity.

Conditions change, but so long as capital exists, profits must be raised and costs reduced. The essence of capitalist cost reduction is routinization and degradation of work. Consider three phases. At the beginning of the Industrial Revolution, handicrafts like weaving and clockmaking were rendered economically useless when the work was mechanized. In the second phase, the middle of industrial capitalism, factory labor shifted from industry to industry, always against a battleground of class struggle over speedup, unsafe working conditions, and (much less contested) the alienation of jobs divided into numbing repetition of the same few motions hour after hour, day after day, year after year.

What happens in the third phase, when the scientific-technical advance of productiveness shrinks industrial labor? In order to continue economic advance with mass prosperity, resources must go into raising the qualification of people for work that requires broad knowledge and judgment, work beyond the capability of the machines of the day. The task is not finished at young adulthood. It is necessary to keep the level of qualification high thereafter, and to requalify people from outmoded areas of competence to new ones. The overall economic process needs to accommodate this allocation of resources. The pinch point of material advance now centers less on resources invested in equipment and more on resources to expand the cultural-productive talents of people. But the overall economic process of capitalism is the accumulation of capital, and labor is a cost to be minimized. Preparation to ever higher cultural levels would usurp the bulk of profit.*

In the twenty years after World War Two, contention in society seemed to compel the allocation of resources in accord with the advance of scientific-technical productiveness. It proved to be a false start. Capital cannot accept human use of a large part of the surplus that is available after current consumption demand is met. It is a direct challenge to the appropriation of profit. When capital cannot invest it all in expansion and advance of production, commercial uses are found for cheap labor, like retail sales and food service, that have little to do with developing powers of production. Luxury consumption expands with the inequality of incomes.

The funds for continually raising the humanity of labor would necessarily be raised by taxes on capital income or by an increase of the cost of employing workers. No, all surplus must stay in the possession of capital, which dominates society by deciding its uses. Capital cannot abide human labor as foretold in nursing and teaching.

Pressure on the mass of workers at the end of the industrial era enables capital to beat down the wages of the most educated workers, too. Youth take on increasingly

---

* Those who try to analyze the breakdown of capitalist accumulation in public are ostracized. However, mass media encourage cynicism with ironic observation of the consequences. Garry Trudeau published a Doonesbury cartoon in which a character says, "Steam power, electrification, industrial farming - they were all disruptive for labor. And yet the great majority of us are still employed. Why? Because each successive advancement liberates us to do higher-valued work." (Doonesbury, May 25, 2014) Cartoonist Trudeau was spared the task of explaining why the great majority of people are employed at increasingly worse jobs.

onerous burdens of debt to get a college degree. U.S. capital prefers that skilled workers be brought in after poorer countries have educated them. Information technology corporations whine that they must have more visas for such workers. They give capable U.S. employees a layoff notice and a final assignment: train a younger, lower-paid replacement to do your job.

Apple, Google, and several other big Silicon Valley corporations colluded to deny wage increases to their employees. The mechanism was a conspiracy not to hire from each other. They coordinated wage schedules. Their engineers have no trade union to bargain as a group. The object of the employers' cabal was to prevent engineers from leveraging their worth to another firm in order to get a better wage. Threats of ruinous hiring contests enforced the conspiracy. When the CEO of Adobe wanted to lure some Apple staff, Steve Jobs shot back, "OK, I'll tell our recruiters they are free to approach any Adobe employee who is not a Sr. Director or VP. Am I understanding your position correctly?" Adobe immediately backed off.[120]

❖

Eras of accumulation are visible from several angles. One is monopoly.

Capitalists hate competition, especially on price. Every capitalist strives for high, secure profits. If strong competition on price breaks out, shrinking the margin of profit, it destroys itself. The weakest firms in the industry go bust. The remaining capitals may agree to a formal cartel, or one firm may achieve a monopoly. Most often, though, a few firms contend against each other within limits while cooperating informally to exclude new competitors. Called an oligopoly, this form of industrial structure combines monopoly and competition.

Every monopoly protects itself by some barrier that excludes new competitors from entering the industry. Economies of scale are the most well-known barrier to entry. In the industrial era, such economies typically required substantial investment in equipment and a large volume of output in order to achieve low cost per item. When one or a few firms produce nearly all the output of an industry, a potential competitor is stymied. It cannot begin with a small output; a company cannot make one thousand cars a year for the mass market at a competitive price. But a large investment, which would need to seize a large share of the market, is risky. The industry remains the preserve of the existing capitals.

Industrial monopolies based on economies of scale and large fixed investments arose in the latter half of the nineteenth century. New methods of production gave rise to new economic relations, in particular, the corporate form of capital ownership and the oligopolies, often called "trusts" at the time, that ran each of the large industries.

Monopoly barriers are never absolute. A new industry may replace one or more old industries, and at the beginning the former is open to new capitals. Occasionally, a monopoly may simply raise prices and margins so high that outside capitals find it worthwhile to push their way in. Competition, understood as the struggle between capitals for the profit, is waged by all sorts of means. Simple price competition is rare, but strategic contention breaks up monopoly, monopoly reappears on new economic terrain, and so it goes.

One reward of monopoly, and one reason that observers across the political spectrum castigate it, may be the ability to retard technological progress. Why spend to make your plant and equipment obsolete? It is still perfectly usable. The products have no replacement – because you refuse to develop them. Just the opposite, you buy up inventions and file them away, hamstring inventors with nuisance patents and litigation, threaten and harass distributors who would carry both your product and a challenger, and use money to enact laws and regulations that establish barriers to entry.

Monopolies may pursue innovations that stimulate sales while suppressing other technology that decreases total revenue or profits. For example, the General Electric Company led the formation in 1924 of the worldwide Phoebus incandescent lighting cartel. The cartel agreed on laws among its members that covered virtually all aspects of the business. Member corporations were permitted to develop bulbs that generated more brightness per watt of electricity. The lumens per watt of a 100-watt tungsten filament bulb rose from 13 in 1924 to 15 in 1935, a minor bit of progress.[121]

The lifetime of a bulb was another matter. In 1933, a GE executive wrote that "the constant reduction of lamp life that we have been in the process of carrying on has kept the volume of business up." A year later the chief executive of Philips bemoaned that other members of the cartel violated the rules on short lamp life under the pressure of the Depression, which had led to "strongly decreased prices in many countries." This was a disaster "after the very strenuous efforts we made to emerge from a period of long life lamps."[122]

Defenders of oligopoly argued that with the available technology, a longer-lasting bulb would consume more electricity per lumen of brightness, raising the cost of il-

130

lumination. We should be thankful for the benevolence of the light bulb monopoly. Yet the cartel did not conduct a research campaign to improve the terms of tradeoff between bulb life and power consumption. Instead, the cartel chose the optimum bulb life not for the consumer's benefit but for maximum sales of replacement bulbs. The price of electricity generally fell, but instead of offering longer-lived bulbs, lifetime was shortened.

GE kept shorter bulb life semi-secret. A GE executive wrote, "The design life of the 2330 Lamp has been changed from 300 back to 200 hours ... no publicity or other announcement will be made of the change."[123] Industrial customers who had the clout to negotiate with GE on bulb life resisted shorter lifetimes. As a GE engineer reported to his boss in 1932, "Two or three years ago we proposed a reduction in the life of flashlight lamps... The battery manufacturers went part way with us on this and accepted lamps of two battery lives instead of three." But the engineer persisted. Lamps that lasted for only one battery change, he enthused, "would result in increasing our flashlight business approximately 60 per cent."[124] Railroads and utilities were able to buy special long-lived lamps that GE made to order for them.[125]

The light bulb oligopoly was in effect when incandescent illumination was mature and a new technology was not ready for industrial development. However, it would be a mistake to think that monopolies always retard innovation. They exist in fields undergoing continual technological innovation, too.

❖

A monopoly based on vigorous scientific research under capitalist direction is pharmaceuticals. From 1960 to 1990, the drug industry ranked first or second in after-tax return on stockholder equity for three of every four years.[126]

The industry owes its existence to chemical scientists like Edward Jenner and Louis Pasteur in the nineteenth century who gave us the germ theory of disease and the first reasonably well-understood vaccines. Spinoffs from research in corporate dyestuff and chemical laboratories (especially German) were important, too. Willow leaf and bark were known as aids in reducing pain five thousand years ago. A scientist produced aspirin, the magic ingredient in them, in 1853, but it was not stable. A chemist in a Bayer laboratory found a way to make pure, stable aspirin that could be manufactured limitlessly.[127]

The drug business was quiescent by the 1930s. A president of Merck said, "You could count the basic medicines on the fingers of your two hands. Morphine, quinine, digitalis, insulin, codeine, aspirin, arsenicals, nitroglycerine, mercurials, and a few biologicals... Most of our products were sold without a prescription. And 43 percent of the prescription medicines were compounded by the pharmacist [at the local drugstore], as compared with 1.2 percent today."[128] Most medicines eased pain; vaccines (among the "biologicals") prevented disease. Drugs could actually treat only a handful of diseases and disorders.

The next phase, stopping diseases that threaten imminent death, would be dramatic. However, we should not forget the background: industrial societies had already extended the average life span by decades, especially by saving babies at birth and preventing death in the first year of an infant's life. It was done with non-drug, largely non-medical measures: clean tap water, safe disposal of sewage in cities, hygiene in the home and sterilization in the hospital, and indoor heating to banish dampness and mold. Vaccines helped, too. Life expectancy at birth in the U.S. was around 35 to 40 years in 1850 (probably less in cities), rising to 48 years in 1900. The largest extension of life was achieved during the first half of the twentieth century, reaching 69 years in 1950. The next half century from 1950, which would see rapid growth of prescription drugs, brought life expectancy to 77 years, a smaller gain and one tempered by problems in the quality of life during the added years.[129]

The pharmaceutical industry we know today came into being around 1950. Its foundation was in place: a quickened pace of underlying science plus three pillars supporting monopoly appropriation of it: expanded patent powers, regulatory approval of drugs after clinical trials, and prescription by physicians. There is almost no regulation of monopoly profits.

The first major antibiotic, penicillin, came from scientists in Britain in the two decades before 1950. They discovered penicillium mold in the laboratory and invented methods of mass producing the drug. Then "Selman Waksman at Rutgers University discovered a technique of screening soil samples to find new antibiotics," working from the insight that harmful micro-organisms do not survive in the ground. "Waksman used his technique to discover the first new antibiotic since penicillin, streptomycin."[130]

Until 1950 the molecular structures of antibiotics were unknown. That year Pfizer contracted with a chemist at Harvard University, who discovered the structure of terramycin. Research expanded from finding potential drugs in the soil to more systematic methods based on X-ray crystallography and spectroscopy, synthesizing candidates in the lab, and testing them. In 1955 Frederick Sanger mapped the amino sequence of insulin, an anti-diabetes medicine used since the early 1920s. Theoretical understanding of how body tissue interacts with bacteria and viruses suggested ways that chemicals might intervene, leading to new drugs.

Shortly after World War Two, the U.S. Patent Office created new "intellectual property," as it is now called. The discovery of a new use for a long-known molecule became eligible for a new patent. Pharmaceutical firms could buy patents and get the exclusive right to make and sell a drug.

A safety law consolidated monopoly possession of a drug emerging out of scientific work. In 1937 a drug company "used diethylene glycol, a sweet-tasting but toxic chemical, to prepare one of the then-new sulfa drugs in syrup form... They did not test it on animals or even review published literature on solvents. After more than 100 people, mostly children, died from the compound, a public uproar prompted rapid approval of the 1938 Food, Drug & Cosmetic Act."[131] Under this law the FDA requires clinical trials of a drug before it is approved for mass consumption. A measure of public protection, spurred by a drug firm's reckless action, also created a barrier to entry for capitals that might aspire to enter the pharmaceutical industry.

Another protection of profits is the requirement that a doctor must prescribe the drug. The pharmaceutical companies built large sales departments staffed by so-called "detail men," who visit doctors and hand out free samples. The corporations backstop their salesmen with intense quasi-scientific advertising to physicians. Existing drug firms spread the costs over their catalog of drugs, while a new firm would have to invest in a similar marketing organization for the sake of one drug.

All in all, the pharmaceutical companies amount to a toll-gate between our ability to advance medicine by scientific work and our enjoyment of medical relief. At the end of the twentieth century (2001) the drug monopolies in the Fortune 500 admitted to as much in a partial breakdown of the shares of their revenue:

Marketing and administration, 30 percent
Profits, 19 percent
Research and development, 13 percent[132]

The heavy toll of marketing expense and profits speaks for itself.

❖

The pharmaceutical industry's mantra is that high profits are necessary to motivate risky research. The cost of research per drug is high, but pharmaceutical corporations overstate the actual expense two to four times. The industry sponsored the most quoted "study" of the high cost of a new drug. The author cherry-picked which drugs to tally and then inflated the outlay by adding a hypothetical amount of opportunity cost.[133]

Even taking industry figures without question, one still finds that the public pays for most of the science through federal funding, while the industry captures the streams of profit. Pharmaceutical corporations depend on research that the federally-funded National Institutes of Health (NIH) sponsor. NIH discovered, developed, and even did the clinical trials that led to the anti-cancer drug Taxol. BristolMyers Squibb licensed it from NIH for a royalty of one-half of one percent of sales. NIH spent $484 million from 1977 to 2002 on the work that created Taxol. No pharmaceutical corporation has the patience to do such long-term research. From 1996 to 2002 BMS paid NIH royalties of $35 million.[134]

We grant a special effort to health – and to the financial prosperity of the industry. The federal government does not have a National Institutes of Transportation Innovation or a National Institutes of Construction.

The federal government obligated itself to pay for more than $28 billion of relevant research in 2009. Research projects in medical science received $11 billion of the total, while broader biological research, excluding agricultural and environmental research, received $17 billion.[135] As the Congressional Budget Office noted, "Only some of that spending is explicitly related to the development of new pharmaceuticals. However, much of it is devoted to basic research on the mechanisms of disease, which underpins the pharmaceutical industry's search for new drugs."[136] The same year the pharmaceutical industry claimed that it spent $45 billion on research and development.[137]

Although universities that benefit from federal grants are no doubt not as efficient and honest as they could be, each research project at the level of basic science is necessarily unsure what results it will produce. The drug industry, though, spends a huge amount of what it classifies as development and research money simply to make profits.

The Food and Drug Administration found in one study that three out of four approved pharmaceuticals "appear to have therapeutic qualities similar to those of one or more already marketed drugs."[138]

Lipitor, Mevacor, Zocor, Pravachol and a couple more drugs are all statins, an anti-cholesterol agent. Compared on what they do, the duplicative cost of tinkering with one or two atoms in the molecular formula and running the variant through clinical tests is mostly waste. Dr. Marcia Angell observed, "Pfizer's Lipitor is the third of three me-too drugs [later there were six variations] to cash in on the success of the first statin, Merck's Mevacor. All of these drugs inhibit the same rate-limiting enzyme in cholesterol synthesis. There is generally no good reason to believe that one me-too drug is better than another, since they are seldom compared head-to-head at equivalent doses in clinical trials."[139]

Each corporation promotes its statin as the best; a major portion of the expense of every drug firm cancels out the same outlay by the other ones. They spend so much on repetitive research and on marketing and selling because this is how they compete with each other, even as the structure and privileges of the industry exclude new capitals.

The long-lived pharmaceutical monopoly is actually a series of rolling monopolies of individual drugs. Each drug has a lifetime gushing profits before it eventually loses patent protection. Even generic drugs have problems from the viewpoint of public interest, such as the practice of the oligopoly brand-name firm paying generic manufacturers a bribe not to make a drug for a few more years.

The drug industry has had an amazing run. From 1947 to 1967, the growth of pharmaceutical shipments outpaced the growth of Gross Domestic Product by 46 percent. During the two decades, production workers as a percentage of total employees fell from 65 to 57 percent. From 1947 all the way to 2009, the growth of industry shipments outpaced GDP by a factor of two and a third.[140] The industry enjoyed extremely rapid growth in demand, yet it excluded significant entry of competitors. What capital would not like to get into an industry with profit rates consistently near the top of the Fortune 500? The drug corporations held the application of science in a fort of patents, regulatory approval, and physician-prescribed sales.

Regulation of the manufacture and sale of pharmaceuticals protects us, but one might suggest that legal limits on drug profits should accompany it. However, it is always difficult to regulate monopoly while respecting, as all respectable reforms must, the sanctity of capitalist property in general. With the state in the hands of capital, regulation ensures the financial health of capital first and the health, more or less, of the population as a justification for the economic regime.

Suppose a rational society required that corporations operate to break even. The sales effort and the duplicative drug development expenditures would shrink enormously. The staff who work in and manage such firms would be rewarded for bringing to market an effective medicine. Drugs would become like aspirin, priced to reflect manufacturing cost, plus a small amount to amortize research expense spread over the volume of pills, injections, and inhalants.

The pharmaceutical monopoly thrives in a peculiar market. The person who chooses whether to prescribe a drug is the doctor, and he does not pay for it. Similarly, many patients who get to a physician have insurance;

they, too, are focused on their health problem, not the cost of the drug. For a broader look at monopoly and technology, we turn to more typical markets and compare a 1970 monopoly with a couple from 2011.

❖

In 1970 Eastman Kodak enjoyed the highest profit margin on sales of the Fortune 100 corporations. The company name shortened to "Kodak" was synonymous with consumer photography. It sold nearly all the film that Americans used for photographs and that Hollywood used for movies. Color film was a curiosity until Kodak introduced its product in the 1930s. Its cameras, from the Brownie at the beginning of the twentieth century to mid-century, and then a series of Instamatic cameras, dominated the snapshot market. Kodak sold film, the paper that photos were printed on, equipment and chemicals for developing photographs, and a host of accessories.

Kodak began in the nineteenth century with chemically coated paper to be used in cameras. It innovated by changing the substrate to transparent cellulose film. George Eastman proposed one of the first corporate laboratories and a program of continuous research and improvement in 1896. He wrote a memo:

"I have come to think that the maintenance of a lead ... will depend greatly upon a rapid succession of changes and improvements, and with that aim in view, I propose to organize the Experimental Department in the Camera Works... If we can get out improved goods every year nobody will be able to follow us and compete with us."[141]

Mr. Eastman was a capitalist, not an innovator for the sake of personal glory, let alone human progress. Kodak

erected a fence of patents around the entirety of photography, excluding almost any threat of competition. His
method of monopoly innovation was similar to contempo-
rary strategy by Goodrich in rubber, General Electric, du
Pont in chemicals, and most prominently the Bell Labs
arm of American Telephone and Telegraph.

To get a taste of the rewards of monopoly based on
technological innovation, compare Eastman Kodak in
1970 with Ford Motor Company. (The year was a good one
for both corporations.) The latter was, and remains, a gar-
den variety oligopoly corporation, number two of the Detroit Three that dominated automobiles.[142] Ford's profit
margin on revenue was 7.3 percent; Kodak raked in an
astounding 29 percent. Kodak's profit per worker was
nearly triple that of Ford, despite the average Kodak employee earning 17 percent more than he or she would get
at Ford. Kodak's plant and equipment yielded profit at a
rate of 31 percent versus 14 percent for Ford.

Anticipating a comparison with four decades later, we
must note how the two firms responded to the income profile of their customers. Ford sold a range of vehicles targeted at different income levels: a Ford for the family of
average income, Mercury above them, and Lincoln for the
highest incomes that still belonged to a mass market. (The
luxury crust buys hand-tooled Ferraris and such.) General
Motors had almost killed Henry Ford's business in the
1920s with model lines targeted to income tiers. Ford's
son Edsel finally got the company to abandon Henry's
edict that one car, the Model T, was good enough for everyone.

Kodak practiced much less income tiering of its cameras and film. This characteristic testifies to the existence
of a broad mass market. A majority of the population

could afford reliable products of acceptable quality for relatively small expenditures like snapshot photography, everyday clothes, and many wares sold in department stores. On the production side of the mass market, Kodak manufactured its products in-house starting from the most basic raw materials. It was a technological corporation, to be sure. Its engineers formulated an enormous library of light-sensitive chemicals. Still, with 111,000 employees worldwide, Kodak was an industrial and commercial employer.

After 1970 both Kodak and Ford were thrown into turmoil. Ford managed to survive as an industrial corporation in the era of accumulation undermined by scientific-technical progress. Kodak did not. In 1970 the company gave up on 35 millimeter single lens reflex cameras. SLR cameras were precision products mostly made in Japan for professional photojournalists and people who aspired to artistic photography, not snaps for the family scrapbook. The Japanese counterpart of Kodak in film, Fujifilm, saw Kodak's huge margins and entered the U.S. market. But it was a fundamental wave of new technology that Kodak could not respond to, digital electronic imaging (even though an engineer in a Kodak research lab had put together one of the first digital cameras). It is not necessary here to play what-if in order to judge whether Kodak's demise was inevitable.

❖

Ford Motor Co. still existed in 2011 as a major industrial corporation in the automotive vehicle oligopoly. To be sure, the oligopoly had gone global. Each year six corporations sell around seventy percent of the cars purchased in the U.S.: General Motors, Toyota, Ford, the Chrysler group, Honda, and Hyundai.[143] The fact that firms headquartered in different countries sell in each others' markets, and the change from the nearly 100 percent U.S. share of the Big Three in the middle of the last century, testify to the change from a series of national oligopolies to one global one.

We compare Ford with a pair of corporations that, as Kodak did, built monopolies based on technological innovation, capturing an outstanding profit margin on sales among the Fortune 100. They are Intel Corp. and Apple Inc., which raked in huge margins of 33 and 32 percent respectively versus Ford's 6.4 percent in 2011. The nearly identical margins (matched, incidentally, by Google, another monopoly) may be a sign that they have reached a limit. If the corporations extracted more, perhaps other capitals could enter the market too easily.

Intel practices innovation like Kodak. It designs, engineers, and largely manufactures its products in house. After decades of globalization, Intel still fabricates 78 percent of its semiconductor products in the United States.[144] Intel's ratio of equipment, plant, and property to revenue is 1.08, similar to Kodak's ratio of 0.92 in 1970.

While both companies maintained monopoly with technological innovation, Intel is in transition away from one practice of the industrial era. It does not take its output all the way to the consumer product. During the desktop and laptop computer era (up to about 2005), Intel and Microsoft dominated choke points along the way to the final product. The pair supplied the microprocessor, the operating system and the basic business software programs, capturing most of the profits from personal computers. Assembler-distributor firms like Compaq, Hewlett Packard, Dell Computer, and some Taiwan companies had the consumer brands but lived on the crumbs for shorter time spans. Intel felt no need to keep computer assembly based on standard labor to itself.

By 2011 Intel was past the height of its most lucrative growth, four decades after its launch in 1968. Although the corporation fabricates processors for tablet computers and smartphones, it does not dominate them as it does desktop and notebook computers. In addition, other firms like Nvidia sliced out a good chunk of graphics processing to the detriment of Intel's processor and chipset product line.

The stark contrast is Apple Inc. It sells a lot of stuff, but it does not supply its so-called solutions to everyone, unlike Kodak in consumer photography. Apple carves out the most expensive 10 to 40 percent of the market in its product categories. Macintosh computers have always been a niche compared with Windows-Intel computers. The iPod is an exception to the pattern, dominating its product category. It redefined mobile music players (a successor to the Sony Walkman) and enjoyed about 75 percent market share. In addition, Apple attempted to monopolize 100 percent of the internet distribution of music via iTunes. In smartphones, Apple's iPhones have a share of about 20 percent by units sold; in tablets, around a third. The corporation's strategy is not to expand downward along the price curve in order to own an entire industry. Instead, the corporation plots its next big product line.

Yet Apple is rarely the vendor to introduce a basic new category of products, although it often garnered the first big success. The company's reputation as a technological innovator is also unearned. Steve Jobs' partner, the ingenious Steve Wozniak, engineered the limited capacities of early personal computer components to do amazing things. The corporation, with Jobs' assent, sidelined Wozniak then encouraged him to depart. Apple scouts new technologies and maneuvers to appropriate them for commercial use, jumping in soon enough to establish a substantial lead.

• Small, high-capacity hard drives made the iPod portable music player possible. After scientists in France and Germany discovered a quantum electronic effect called giant magnetoresistance, and after the Department of Energy funded additional work at its laboratory in Illinois, researchers at IBM's Almaden, California laboratory applied the effect to hard drive storage. Apple simply bought the drives.[145]

• Apple's iPhone popularized the "swipe" and other multi-touch gestures on touchscreens. A graduate student and professor at the University of Delaware created the technology then put it in a company called FingerWorks. Apple bought FingerWorks two years before it introduced the iPhone.[146]

• Stanford Research Institute coordinated government-supported development of intelligent voice recognition among teams at twenty universities. SRI formed the SIRI company and sold it, with the technology of the same name, to Apple in 2010.[147]

The company does deserve its reputation for sleek boxes, an undeviating focus on simplicity of use, and bold, shallow advertising.

Apple is what Cadillac, the upper tier of automobiles, might look like if it had remained an independent company from its founding in 1903. However, Cadillac merged five years later into what was to become General Motors.

In addition, there would be no Lincoln, no Chrysler Imperial, and no Toyota Lexus. Apple drives to monopolize a premium price range within a product category. It does so with industrial design, selective materials like the glass on most of its iPhones that are guarded by exclusive contracts with suppliers (Corning supplied the special glass), and packs of lawyers ready to fight over intellectual property.

Apple certainly leverages market clout with old-fashioned tactics. The iPod music player was crippled so that users could download music for it only from Apple's online iTunes outlet. Apple took about a third of the 99-cent price for serving a file download that probably cost less than a penny. Apple tried to dominate e-books in a similar ploy with the iPad tablet, but the scheme was too bold. The federal government could not overlook the antitrust violations. The company has its eyes on the distribution of television programs, too.

It is all lucrative beyond belief. Although Apple's margin on sales is almost the same as Intel's, its profit margin on investment in fixed assets was 291 percent in 2011, compared with 31 percent at Intel and 18 percent at Ford Motor Co. Nor does Apple need many workers. Sales per employee in 2011 were $1.6 million at Apple, versus $540,000 at Intel and $831,000 at Ford.

The gigantic ratios testify not only to Apple's high-end products and prices. The millions of smartphones, tablets and computers must be assembled, and their parts must be manufactured with substantial equipment. Apple, however, disdains investment in such operations. A teardown of an iPhone 3G found that Toshiba supplied the flash memory along with the display and touch screen modules; Samsung made the processor and the dynamic random access memory; and other companies provided the remainder of the electronics, the case, and so on. Apple is able to muscle suppliers, high tech and low tech alike. They all shipped their output to the contract assembly factories where Chinese workers put together the iPhone.[148] Apple has a substantial number of employees, 67,000*, but several times that number of workers toil in factories run on much smaller margins that Apple itself takes.

❖

The contrast between Kodak and Apple testifies to their different economic environments. Kodak was a technological innovator in the industrial era; Apple is a product designer in the scientific-technical era of capitalism. A relatively uniform mass market thinned in the middle and swelled at the extremes. At one end are the increasing number of people who have a life worse than their parents; at the other end are people who prefer and can afford premium items, at least for something that costs only a tenth or a twentieth of a basic automobile. The Apple monopoly is narrower than what Kodak had yet more lucrative.

Apple revenues, $108 billion in 2011, rival Ford Motor's $136 billion that year. To get that additional quarter of revenue, Ford had nearly two and half times as many employees and more than four times as much money sunk into plant and equipment.

Ford was the base company for comparison with extraordinary monopolies in 1970 and 2011, but it, too,

---

* They divide between technical professionals and a sales force in the company's retail stores, with few in between.

changed. Vehicle production in 2011, 5.7 million, was a quarter more than the 4.5 million cars and trucks it produced in 1970, yet Ford needed 431,000 employees then but only 164,000 in 2011. The corporation shed 60 percent of its workers, partly by adopting robots and other automation, partly by contracting out the manufacture of individual parts and entire subassemblies like the front and back seat modules. Some of Ford's suppliers increased automation, too; some are outright sweatshops. The reduction of Ford employees by 267,000 dwarfs the number who hold jobs at Apple.

The big story in the appearance of more selective monopolies is not so much the monopolies themselves. They exist within the general application of scientific-technical advance that raises productiveness and ousts workers from middle-income jobs without creating comparable new jobs. Where are those 267,000 workers and their children? With rare exceptions, they do not work at Apple Inc., Google, and other Silicon Valley marvels. They slog on in warehouses, offices, factories, and retail outlets at pay debased from the wages of 1970 automobile plants, with little job security, puzzling over a retirement plan, if any, that is subject to sudden financial gyrations, and looking at even dimmer prospects for their children.

We expect that science-based technology should make life better. Disappointment of the expectation generates a dystopian attitude to science and technology, accusing them of being founts of oppression and of detaching reason from human values. In between enthusiasm for scientific wonders and deeply disappointed assessments is the moderate's view that the prudent social policies can prevent undesirable consequences of technology while enabling it to deliver benefits widely. All three attitudes are mistaken. They are imbued with the prevailing non-class outlook on social life.

The core of the economic process is not technology but the antagonism of profit for capital versus the needs of workers. Employees are a cost to capital, and costs must be reduced to survive, to expand and to vanquish other capitals rather than be wiped out. The three non-class attitudes tend to ponder technological objects as realizations of ideas, isolating technology from labor.

Many utopians, centrists, and dystopians sympathize with assembly workers in electronics sweatshops. They mislead themselves with statistics that paying assembly employees a better wage, relaxing the intense work pace, and curtailing the 60- and 70-hour workweeks would add only several dollars to the price of the final product. True. Equally true is the fact that those sweated dollars constitute the profit of contract assembly capitals. Foxconn was the lead assembly company for Apple iPhones and iPads in the years 2008 to 2011. During that period Foxconn's operating margin was never higher than four percent; sometimes it was as low as one percent. Apple margins fluctuated between 15 and 33 percent. Of course, when an assembly firm has one million employees and most of them work with hand tools, the owners make a fortune on even a small margin.[149]

Technological monopolies like Kodak, Intel, and Apple are an instance of the fact that we can understand technology, and new productive methods in general, only in their subordinate relation to profit. Capital will certainly turn to new products and productive methods. The use of them must be according to the nature of the technology, but the technology is confined within the orbit of accumulation. The evolution from Kodak to Apple is an example of the reciprocal interaction. Kodak exploited a technological niche during the industrial era of a broad mass market. Apple exploits a niche of major technologies during an era of scientific-technical development, increasing inequality, and contradictions in capitalist accumulation.

❖

Apple enjoys a premium market position; things are different in the general mass market. Consider Costco and Walmart, two large retailers operating big stores. Costco pays better than Walmart. Hourly wages for front-line clerks and cashiers rises in a few years to levels well above Walmart. The health plan premium for Costco employees is about 12 percent, versus 40 percent for those Walmart employees who can afford it.[150] Costco provides additional generous benefits. Both companies are profitable, so why can't Walmart be like Costco?

The decisive point for capital is that Walmart makes much more profit out of its business than Costco. In 2007-08 before the depths of the recession, Walmart's pre-tax profit margin on sales was 5.3 percent, nearly twice Costco's 2.8 percent. Some of the difference is because of the fact that Costco is more grocery-centric, a business with lower margins than general goods. Still, when it comes to investing capital, the difference is clear: Walmart's return on total assets was 12.4 percent versus 9.7 percent at Costco; return on equity was 31.3 percent versus 21.6 percent.[151] If buyout investors contemplate the numbers, they ask themselves, how could we raise the returns at Costco?

Suppose the Costco executives woke up one morning and found themselves in Bentonville, Arkansas in charge of Walmart. They could not announce that the employees would now receive Costco-level wages and benefits. Big stockholders would scream about the "fiduciary responsibility" to maximize profits. Nor could the executives argue that workers would increase their productivity. Costco employees know they have a relatively good job for general retail, that is, in comparison with the likes of Walmart, Dollar Tree and so on. When people work at Costco, they tacitly agree to supervise themselves and take care of things that a Walmart employee is too rushed to stop and fix.

Perhaps Walmart executives considered whether they could earn the same profits with fewer but better-paid workers. If so, the answer is apparently no. Of course, managers continually review whether the stores can run with fewer workers, period. In fact, the business press reported in 2013 that Walmart had cut staff hours so deeply that there is often no one to restock shelves. Empty shelves mean lost sales. The bosses dropped a rock on their own feet.

4.

Socialism Develops

The disruptions of capitalist accumulation hollow out a colossus that grew for 400 years. It also hardens the terms of class struggle. Working people no longer expand the dimensions of mass prosperity; they fight to slow its disappearance.

Workers must always fight for better wages and more human working conditions. Class struggle is inherent in capitalism, and capital has the upper hand. The relation of one capital to each of many workers is tilted. An individual employee's power to hold out for a better wage, or resist a cutback, is usually no match for an employer's power to replace the employee. Collective struggle, from spontaneous moments of unity among the staff to organized trade unions, is the only way to get a more even-handed bargain between one employer and its workers, or between the employers and employees of an industry. The economic struggle spills into the political arena, too. Both classes want to write rules for the job market, and they contend over how much of a safety net unemployed, disabled, and other workers will have.

151

Although capital has the house advantage, it does not win every deal of the cards. The economic situation conditions the strength of capital and workers, and the outcome of struggles between them reacts on the economic situation. The dominant force is the state of capitalist accumulation. We saw this fact when we examined the cycle of prosperity and slump, beginning from the distinction between genuine full employment and capitalist full employment.

The economic situation sets limits on the possibilities of class struggle over the terms of employment. Working people may turn to struggle aimed at the overthrow of capitalism. For now, we consider only economic class struggle, which includes political battles to extract labor and social reforms from the capitalist state.

The sustained campaign in the United States for unions appropriate to the industrial era was won during the 1930s, after about 60 years of struggle over the consequences of large factories, assembly lines, and monopoly trusts and corporations. The goal was defined: a union for all the workers in an industry, with a contract to be continually enforced and improved from term to term. The concept was opposed both to the craft union that divided the workers confronting an employer by divisions of skill as well as to the organizing model of the Wobblies (Industrial Workers of the World, or I.W.W.), which was as episodic as it was heroic.[152]

Establishment historians attribute legal trade unions to the Wagner Act of 1935, which expanded section 7(a) of the National Industrial Relations Act of 1933. The statutes did not create the unions. Rather, mass movement for unions prompted the statutes, which graciously allowed them and attempted to formalize their rights and responsibilities. It was still up to the workers to defeat employers' resistance. The high points were the sitdown strikes of 1936-37 and armed attacks by the second tier of steel corporations, which delayed their unionization to 1942 but taught many people what an enemy business is. From 1930 to 1940 the number of union members jumped from fewer than three and a half million to almost nine million workers.[153]

There were always two institutional styles of industrial unions, business unionism and what is today called social unionism. Running the union as a business means confining it to pursue the best contract for the members, plus legislation in support of that aim. Social unionism takes a wider view of the labor market, since workers move between industries and their children enter new industries. Social unions insist on an open door and equality in their ranks, not exclusion from membership with racist, ethnic, and familial patronage barriers. Social unionism joins struggles for unemployment insurance, against discrimination, and for higher education on a mass scale.

The distinction is clear in the example of health care. Social unionists support guaranteed care for all, for example, an improved Medicare program extended to everyone regardless of age. Business unions like to put health insurance in their contracts because it ties the members to the union and is a selling point if they conduct an organizing drive. Business unions see themselves as a walled-off group interest, not as a contingent of a class. It is divisive: we have something you don't have.

Congress seriously considered national health insurance in 1948. Despite the negotiation of company plans during World War Two as a way around wage controls, a survey that year found that most labor leaders opposed collectively-bargained pensions and health plans, implicitly supporting a national health insurance program. However, business unionist Phil Murray, joined by John L. Lewis and Walter Reuther, committed the steelworkers, miners, and autoworkers unions to company and industry health plans.[154]

The same opposed approaches to class struggle reflect within social unionism itself. At one end, social democrats believe that capitalism can provide a good life for workers and that most capitalists can be brought to realize this alleged truth. Campaigns may be waged to achieve agreements with capital along these lines. Despite the label, social democrats are against struggle for socialism, although they confuse the issue in ways that need not detain us here.

At the other end of this opposition, social realists hold that the antagonism of interests between capital and the working class is irreconcilable. Battles for the maximum gain now must be conducted in light of the basic goal of replacing capitalism with socialism. This outlook strengthens union action: social realists are usually better strategists, more dedicated fighters, and, ironically, more democratic about winning members' commitment to a course of action.[155] For the moment, we can note a point of unity: social realists reject narrow craft unions and business unionism, and social democrats often did, too.

Once industrial unions became a reality shortly before World War Two, many capitalists came to appreciate that they could help tamp down conflict in the workplace. A labor contract typically enlisted union officers to prevent and stop wildcat strikes. Still, capital was not happy about the militancy and seemingly endless vision of a better life that workers acquired in the course of stormy union campaigns.

Soon after World War Two ended, it was time to discipline labor with a good dose of repression. Capital, supported by business unionists, confined trade unions to narrow limits of action. The Taft-Hartley Act of 1947 made wildcat strikes outright illegal along with various forms of worker solidarity on picket lines. In addition, the Act required trade union leaders to swear affidavits that they were not communist. President Truman gave a signal early in 1947 when he ordered a loyalty check of every federal employee. You did not need to be a Communist with a capital C for the government and top union officials to brand you a communist. If you were militant, you were a target. The FBI spoke to your employer, who found reason to fire you. If you had been elected to union office, higher-up officials ousted you.

The repression broadened. Civil rights leaders and groups were disciplined for unacceptable militancy. So were peace activists who ventured that U.S. imperialism had something to do with war after war in the colonies and with the tense standoff that threatened global nuclear annihilation. If you had a public presence as a progressive artist, entertainer, or writer, you were excluded from work in theatres, Hollywood movies, radio, television, books and magazines.*

---

* Senator Joe McCarthy was a latecomer when he took up red-baiting in 1950 to boost his political career. The core of the militant left had already been repressed. He was a flash in the pan, too. Anti-communist smears and repression were used

The Congress of Industrial Organization tossed out numerous trade unions, split others, and purged a wide swath of union militants in the postwar anti-communist campaign that accompanied Taft-Hartley. The uneasy balance between social unionism and business unionism in the 1930s was resolved in favor of the latter. A watered-down version of social unionism was allowed to tag along for show. Walter Reuther was the major practitioner of talking like a social unionist while undercutting its thrust again and again.

This was the state of economic class struggle when trade union and political forces had to grapple with the transformation of capital accumulation from an industrial to a scientific-technical basis.

❖

In the early 1950s automation confronted industrial workers. The defeat of social unionism left trade unions unable to do much about it, certainly in business union contracts. The ostracism of social realists made it more difficult for trade unions to understand the momentous change in capital accumulation. This handicap was one of the consequences of the anti-communist drive of the late 1940s that would hamper workers right up to our time.

In the short run, things did not seem so bad. Real wages rose, with cyclical interruption, for twenty more years. The worker in the middle of the income distribution got the highest wage in real dollars that he would ever obtain under capitalism. High school education became uni-

---

against wider circles of liberal and mildly radical activists and cultural workers to the end of the 1950s.

versal (except for Black people) . Then a vast expansion of two-year community colleges seemed to foreshadow the day of full higher education for workers' children. Union leaders enjoyed comfortable collaboration with capital most of the time. It was not heavenly peace, to be sure. Strikes, somewhat ritualized like a church service, occurred fairly regularly. The steelworkers waged a 116-day strike in 1959.

No doubt some union leaders became upset as they realized that membership peaked in 1956 both in absolute numbers and as a percentage of the workforce.[156] But what to do?

Conscious struggle lags behind the incessant change of material realities. The accumulation of capital entered a fundamentally new phase around 1973, but in the next few years, no social force recognized it. Neither capital nor organized labor introduced a new phase of class struggle. There was an important burst of wildcat sickouts and strikes in the late 1960s and early 1970s in automobile factories, but they were confined to an episode. It is difficult to recognize a deep change until some time after it is well in place.

The underlying change in accumulation affected use of the strike, the essential weapon of struggle over wages. It stops the flow of revenue and raises costs. So long as the possibility of a strike is serious, the union has clout in negotiations.

In 1973, unannounced, the strike weapon began to lose its strength, like a wooden beam rotted by fungus. From 1950 the number of days workers were out on work stoppages had risen gradually. (See trend line through ups and downs in the figure.) Every few years the number of

157

days on strike jumped sharply, probably because several major contracts expired together.)[157] The spike in 1974 might have been reassuring, but the trend from then to 1990 was sharply down, cutting the average number of days out in half. Then strikes nearly disappeared. The 1997 strike at United Parcel Service and the Verizon strike of 2000 stand as heroic exceptions.

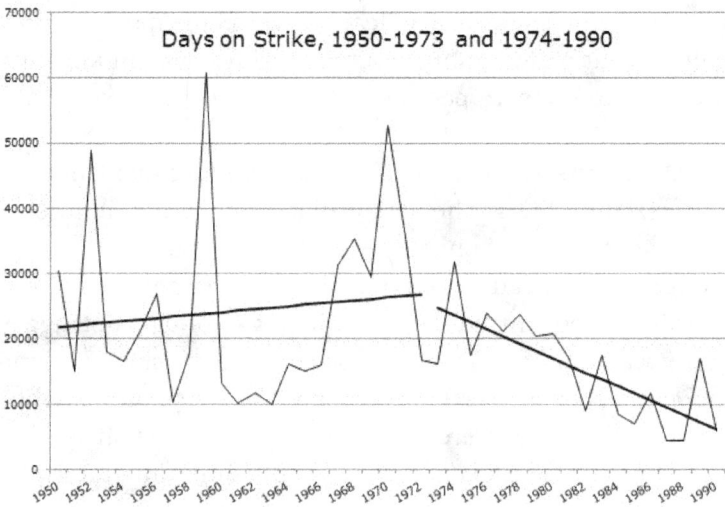

Days on Strike, 1950-1973 and 1974-1990

Generally, a successful strike requires that union leaders and activists make a careful assessment and decide what is winnable. The union evaluates the factors confronting capital: how much revenue will the employer lose, how much will post-strike animosity cost in day-to-day productiveness, what new business beckons? On the union side, the majority of members must vow that the sacrifice of a strike is worthwhile and necessary. Well in advance of a strike, activists ponder what must be done to solidify the members' cohesion and commitment as well as community support. Also, how big is the strike fund? Even when a union does all it can to gather power, the test is always the economic and political "lay of the land" at the moment of decision: the overall economy, the prosperity of the industry, and the situation of the employer.

Capital did not legislate the 1973 turning point from a routine level of strike activity to its virtual elimination as the workers' weapon in the economic struggle. To be sure, capital will outlaw when it so decides. The Taft-Hartley Act of 1947 openly announced that the government would no longer tolerate substantial expansion of unions.

Nor did trade union officials consciously set a new practice of fewer strikes, no matter how much they were steeped in business unionism.

The statistics are the sum of many contract situations, each decided on its particular circumstances. Strikes stopped happening because a turn in accumulation changed the struggle at the workplace. Unions and corporate labor executives could see the consequences in each organizing drive and each contract struggle, but not much deeper. When you pilot a ship on the ocean, you can learn a lot from an experienced look at the surface of the water, but eyesight will not tell you that a major current near the bottom of the sea changed course.

❖

Labor officials and activists looked for alternatives to the strike. Consumer boycotts, corporate campaigns appealing to public opinion, legislation that would at least tolerate collective bargaining and union organizing – all were tried. Despite occasional successes, unions found no substitute.

Social democrats in the labor movement are in a bind. On one hand, they recognize that traditional union methods of struggle no longer win significant gains, even while they remain part of the defense against an increasingly savage capitalist class. On the other hand, social democrats are reluctant to admit that capitalism can no longer deliver both profits for capital and a degree of mass prosperity. The traditional social democratic line was that the capitalists must be pushed to prosperity for both classes. Indeed, "win-win" was possible in industrial capitalism, although partial and unstable. It will never be true of capitalism again.

Deep economic change undermined strikes, the core element of trade union power. A social democratic analyst has a different explanation: "At stake in labor's decline is, in addition to its economic character, nothing less than the political and social climate of American society. That we have growing inequality in America – income differences are greater than in any advanced industrial society – may be ascribed mainly to the erosion of trade union power rather than to some mysterious market mechanism."[158]

When Stanley Aronowitz refers with sarcasm to "some mysterious market mechanism," he mocks neoliberal worship of unregulated capital. The problem is the other end of his "rather than." For Aronowitz, the erosion of trade union strength is a principal cause of the economic change rather than one of its effects. He does not see how fundamental developments in accumulation and production weaken standard labor. These explain the erosion of trade union power, the stagnation of the real median wage, and the growth of income inequality.

Aronowitz is an interesting social democratic commentator because he tackles the problem of automation. "Powerful unions did win a fairly substantial share of the cost savings produced by automation, but their deals do much to explain why wages and salaries have declined steadily since the early 1970s. Many sons and daughters of union members can no longer follow their parents into the well-paid union job; instead, they are obliged to seek work in low-wage, nonunion retail and service jobs, which typically pay half what factory and transportation jobs pay."[159] He is wrong on two counts. The coal miner and dockworker contracts that accepted automation in return for payouts to current members may deserve harsh criticism – but Aronowitz loads far too much weight on them. We should not entangle the question of whether unions in general were as militant as be with how several unions negotiated a handful of contracts to deal with technological changes.[160]

Second, Aronowitz goes beyond calling for more militant trade union action. He believes unions could have maintained the relative mass prosperity of the first postwar decades. It is the social democratic illusion of compelling capitalism to deliver both profits to capital and a better life to workers.

Capitalism no longer functions that way. Trade unions with fight in them might have slightly delayed the fundamental decline that began in 1973 – no more. Certainly, vigorous struggle is better than accommodation. For one thing, experience shows that a good fight wins more than a request to collaborate with capital. Equally important, struggle teaches us what we are up against; people see their exhilarating strength when they act together for class interest; and new commitment, understanding, and organization open the way to even stronger action.

Social democrats welcome Aronowitz's analysis because it poses the task of reviving trade union power within capitalism. In his formulation, trade union power in the struggle over the terms of employment and accompanying social legislation is everything. In reality, the power of the working class is to remake society. As capitalism decays, recognition of the need to exercise this power awakens.

With deft straddling, Aronowitz writes a few pages later, "After 1973 union bargainers could no longer rely on the growth and stability of the nation's economy to justify their wage and benefits demands; European and Asian competitors and a number of transnational corporations prompted employers to insist that labor become competitive with itself."[161] He more or less concedes that unions had a big problem in the objective situation, not only in officials' absence of will. However, he substitutes narrative for explanation, alluding to world competition against U.S. capital. We saw earlier that global competition does not explain why capitalist growth faltered in Europe and Japan as well as the U.S.

Aronowitz writes, "Much of the marxist tradition has come to view the productive forces as the motive power of historical change."[162] Actually, the motive power of historical change is the ever-evolving contradiction between the productive forces (the equipment, the technology it embodies, the knowledge, and skills used to produce things) and the relations of production (the relations between people, especially between classes, within which production is carried out). We have entered the time under capitalism when the class struggle for gains within this contradiction becomes continually more difficult. Class struggle is driven toward breaking up the capitalist relations of production.

❖

The capitalist class did not understand things better than anyone else. They could not get beneath a host of problems facing them in the early 1970s. This was the last phase of the Black people's civil rights struggle, in the aftermath of the 1965 Watts riot and the 1967 uprisings in Detroit, Newark and ghettos across the country. A prolonged mass movement still opposed the U.S. war in Vietnam. Women launched their own liberation movement, including equal pay for equal work. Counterculture assaulted prevailing arts and entertainment, although artists had to choose whether to reconstruct the cultural establishment or win a niche within it. These upsurges won important advances of democratic rights; eventually, the ruling elite found way to co-opt them and apply the brakes.

A problem remained that capitalists diagnosed and discussed among themselves. It was the biggest threat to profits. In 1971 Lewis Powell wrote a memo for the U.S. Chamber of Commerce, intended to be secret though soon discovered and published, about "The Attack on the Free Enterprise System." (President Nixon nominated Powell to the Supreme Court two months later.) What was this attack and who was behind it?

Powell did not see a threat from the labor movement. The memo makes one small, neutral comment about trade unions. Like other interest groups, "labor unions insist that textbooks be fair to the viewpoints of organized labor ... In a democratic society, this can be a constructive process."[163] Powell accepts the debate, urging corporations to jump into it. Nor was Powell worried about "Communists, New Leftists and other revolutionaries who would destroy the entire system, both political and economic... they remain a small minority, and are not yet the principal cause for concern."[164]

It did upset Powell that a poll of college students at a dozen supposedly representative campuses reported, "Almost half the students favored socialization of basic U.S. industries."[165] Certainly, he wanted to hold the ideological line, but the crucial problem for free enterprise was not really a contest between capitalism versus socialism.

Instead, Powell raised his rifle of a pen and drew aim on "the single most effective antagonist of American business" – Ralph Nader! Powell quoted Milton Friedman, who was horrified at the object "of his [Nader's] hatred, which is corporate power." Nader did not confine himself to exposing small-fry hucksters; he believes that many in "the top management of blue-chip business ... belong in prison."[166]

Capital was accustomed to producing what it wanted, how it wanted. It sold accident-ready cars and other dangerous products to uninformed consumers. It ordered workers to handle hazardous materials without safeguards. It polluted the air, rivers, and lakes.

Ralph Nader was the spark and the leader of a broad movement for regulation in the interests of ordinary people. He and other "enemies" of free enterprise demanded that corporations disclose what they do and obey some laws when they produce and sell, just as ordinary people must obey traffic laws when they get behind the wheel. Thanks to Nader and those who worked with him we got the Environmental Protection Agency (1970); the Occupational Safety and Health Act (1970); the Consumer Product Safety Commission (1972); legal protections for credit card holders; and major improvements of the laws on Freedom of Information (1974), Clean Water (1972) and Clean Air (1970).

Powell characterized such regulation as nothing less than "warfare against the enterprise system and the values of western society."[167] He directed capitalists' attention to the shackles of regulation and called for a fight against it. They took action, whether because they heard Powell's alarm or because they independently recognized a growing need to capture profits by shaping governmental policy as much as by winning in the market. "In 1971, only 175 firms had registered lobbyists in Washington, but by 1982, nearly 2,500 did. The number of corporate PACs increased from under 300 in 1976 to over 1,200 by the middle of 1980. On every dimension of corporate political activity, the numbers reveal a dramatic rapid mobilization of business resources in the mid-1970s."[168]

No major social-economic reform has been enacted since the worker safety, consumer, and environmental protections won in the Nixon years. These were the last chapter after Medicare (1965), the social welfare programs of the 1960s, and the trade union, unemployment, and Social Security gains of the 1930s.

Meanwhile, corporations tolerated business unionism (while resisting attempts to unionize) for almost a decade

after Powell's memo, after the downtrend of work stoppages, after the peak of worker's wages, and well into the
passage from viable industrial accumulation to deeply
contradictory scientific-technical development.

Finally, in August 1981 President Reagan officially re-
pealed the postwar relationship between capital and the
trade unions. Air traffic controllers needed shorter hours
and better equipment as a remedy for overwork, caused to
a large degree by airline deregulation during the preceding
Carter administration. The Professional Air Traffic Controllers Organization (PATCO) went on strike against the
Federal Aviation Administration after slowdowns and
sickouts brought no relief. Reagan fired the 11,345 controllers on strike. Furthermore, he hired scabs not only to
break the strike (with the aid of controllers from the military) but as permanent replacements. He banned the fired
controllers from ever working at the FAA again. Reagan, a
former president of the Screen Actors Guild, destroyed
PATCO as an organization.

Corporate executives saw Reagan's green light. Hiring
permanent replacements during strikes became accepted
practice. The core of neoliberalism, traditionally dated
from the early 1980s, is the drive to push working people
down without limit. After 1981 the rate of decline in strike
activity became somewhat more rapid. What actually collapsed from that year was the workplace vote in which
employees decided whether or not they would have a union. Within three years the number of elections held under
the auspices of the National Labor Relations Board fell almost in half.[169]

❖

After forty-plus years of stagnant and falling real earnings of workers, the conclusion is inescapable: mass prosperity is no longer possible within capitalism. We must consider what comes next. Almost everyone knows the common name for the economic order that challenges capitalism – socialism. But what is it?

There are many answers, too many. Marx and Engels devoted a chapter of the *Communist Manifesto* to a mocking catalog of varieties like feudal socialism, petty bourgeois socialism, and bourgeois socialism. They did so to help show that socialism emerges as a serious program for a new economic order with the birth of the industrial working class in the late eighteenth century. It is the banner of workers aspiring to be the first non-exploitive ruling class. Socialism is so attractive that spokespersons of other classes try to appropriate its aura and convince workers to support a non-socialist or anti-socialist program.

A more acid fog envelopes the term communism. We use it to refer to movements, parties, and countries that pursue socialism based on scientific analysis of an economy according to its relations of labor and its productive powers. We set aside the other principal use of the word, which reserves communism to name the stage of society after socialism. Of course, it is irrelevant whether a political group puts "Communist" in its name.

While the class character of socialism is set, its economic content changes with the development of the capitalism that socialism demands to replace. Several prominent examples illustrate the varying content. One is the 1917 revolution and construction of socialism in the Soviet Union; the Chinese case is closely related. Another example is the European and U.S. working class movements of the nineteenth and twentieth centuries, a portion of which was communist. Our time discovers a third stage of economic content.

The problem in Russia was industrialization. It was obvious by comparison with England, Germany, France, and so on. In 1917 there were three million workers among a population of 145 million. The working class was concentrated in large factories (one thousand workers or more) to a greater degree than the United States. Still, eight out of ten people were peasants, and 30,000 large landowners exploited them. The capitalist class was incapable of leading a revolution against the tsar, hoping instead to win a place alongside the land-based aristocrats in a reformed monarchy. Then industrialization could proceed over a span of fifty years, similar to Japan after the so-called Meiji Restoration. Although a few tsarist officials were of similar mind, notably the police-state expert Peter Stolypin, the regime did not budge.

The working class made the 1917 revolution and proceeded to tackle industrialization run by the working class for the benefit of the working people. One of V. I. Lenin's famous declarations is, "Communism is Soviet power plus the electrification of the whole country." It is instructive to read his 1920 remark with more context: "We are not dismayed by our having to repeat the basic axioms of economic development... Communism is Soviet power plus the electrification of the whole country... we shall see to it that the economic basis is transformed from a small-peasant basis into a large-scale industrial basis."[170] Lenin died in 1924 at age 53. After several years of debate, the

Communist Party of the Soviet Union decided on a policy of rapid industrialization.

Socialist industrialization included a whole range of social welfare measures. There was no unemployment. The working class, absorbing millions of peasants to build new factories and run them, accomplished the job in the ten years leading up to World War Two. Because of this achievement the Soviet Union smashed the Nazi drive to global barbarism.

In China, too, the problem of the revolution was industrialization. After three thousand years of agrarian dynasties, the country would start from a point of even less economic development than tsarist Russia.

The long chain of Chinese emperors snapped with a light yank in 1911, but large landowners, big bourgeoisie, and warlords (served by the Chiang Kai-shek regime) showed they would not allow a thriving modern country. The Communist Party became the center for all who wanted to modernize. The workers and peasants were ready to fight, and the Party transformed millennia of peasant rebellion into people's war.* The appeal of the Party was extraordinarily wide. Among better-off provincial families, education of sons for a government post was a venerable strategy.[171] Now, the head of a modestly prosperous peasant or small landlord family might send one son into the ruling Kuomintang and another son into the Communist Party.

The Communist Party led a peasant army to liberate China. They succeeded in 1949. For a quarter century af-

---

* This invention was possible because the leaders, especially Mao Zedong, had the methods of historical materialism and dedicated themselves to integrating with the peasants.

ter that, the Chinese people worked hard to lay the foundations of industrial prosperity for all. Every major government decision was difficult, however. Two sides contended over socialist industrialization versus capitalist industrialization. When the pro-capitalist group led by Deng Xiaoping took over in 1978, two years after the death of Mao Zedong, development took off because the paralyzing dispute was settled and because the people had already built an enormous infrastructure: near-universal basic schooling, mass literacy, irrigation works, terraced hills and other farmland improvements, the beginnings of basic industry, and more.

The socialist Soviet Union and China did not pioneer industrialization. They saw what productive advance was possible by the example of other countries in Europe and North America and to some extent Japan. Communists in the two countries took the momentous step of conceiving of revolution to overthrow agrarian rule and then proceed to socialist industrialization. They carried out this program, breaking with Menshevik (social democratic) dogma. That latter held that since the industrial complex of productive forces had first appeared in history as capitalism, therefore socialists must stand aside after an anti-feudal revolution and leave industrialization to capital in every country. The Bolshevik policy – unitary planning of the national economy and administrative coordination of industries – proved to be a successful method of socialist industrial development.

Communists did face a new historical problem, that of bringing along most of the peasants. When capitalist economies industrialize, they brutally drive peasants and farmers off the land. A peasant's first idea of liberation is that his family gets a chunk of land to farm as its own, freed of paying heavy taxes and fees to a landlord and local aristocrats. Socialist industrialization would eventually draw most of the peasants' children and grandchildren into the working class. During that time the communists had to convince peasants through their own experience that progress lay in combining tiny plots of land and working it in collectives. At first, teams were bigger than a family, then they were wider than a village. Larger scale made it easier to use tractors and other machines as they became available.

Socialism had a definite program for the benefit of the working people: industrialization without income for landed and capitalist property. The program corresponded to the productive level of the society, broke up the class relations that denied a decent life to the working masses, and achieved rapid economic progress.

Capitalist commentators tell all sorts of fabrications about the Soviet Union during the time of Lenin and Stalin and about China during the era of Mao Zedong. Are we surprised that a chihuahua dog squawks? It is not necessary to refute gutter writers here. We should note, however, that they intend to do more than enforce a historical verdict. They want to close the book on socialism forever. The fact that history often moves two steps forward and one step back helps them. These socialist societies made tremendous advances while under continuous pressure, internal and external. They fell to capitalist restoration after thirty to forty years. The socialist project is essentially historical, confronting new conditions. It remains the banner of the working class determined to put an end to exploitation.

❖

Industrialization in western Europe and in the United States got underway in the late eighteenth and early nineteenth century, long before the working class movement had a significant communist contingent. Industrial expansion brought the working class to a substantial size and cohesion, and socialist aspirations grew large.

There were no successful revolutions in these regions during the industrial era, but revolutionary aspirations of the people burst forth from time to time:

• The working class revolted in 1871 during a war between France and Prussia, set up the Paris commune, and ran the city for two months.[172] Karl Marx had written in an 1852 letter that one of his three original contributions to the science of history was to prove "that the class struggle necessarily leads to the dictatorship of the proletariat" and then to a society without classes. He celebrated the Commune as the first example.[173]

• A revolution broke out in Germany in November 1918 (as well, half of all French soldiers had joined mutinies in May and June 1917, and there were scattered mutinies of British troops later that year). The imperialist powers quickly brought World War One to an end, enabling German officers to crush the revolution. The next year a revolutionary government was set up briefly in Hungary.

• At the end of World War Two, the Communist Parties of France and Italy assessed the chances of revolution, concluding they were good but not strong enough to risk the possible consequences for the Soviet Union. They might have figured higher odds for success if Winston Churchill had been able to launch his Operation Unthinkable. He dreamed of sending two and half million troops to start a war against the Soviet Union on July 1, 1945 and "impose upon Russia the will of the United States and British Empire."[174]

• In 1968 a general strike and factory occupations all across France signaled that workers were ready for more. President de Gaulle made a clandestine emergency visit to a top French general in Germany, confirming that he would get military aid to suppress the French people.[175] The Communist Party, rotten by then, not only provided no leadership; its factory leaflets slandered the college students whose rebellions had given workers their opening.

Industrial capitalism never fell to revolution in its heartlands, but class struggle raged over wages, the length of the workday, the right to form trade unions and bargain collectively with the employer, free public education, unemployment insurance, welfare and safety legislation, universal health care, and more.* Adherents of socialism were the most active people in these struggles. They also opposed imperialist wars and defended countries fighting for liberation. They were the first victims when capitalist states tossed aside democracy and resorted to fascism.

The content of the socialist program in this era was continued industrialization without capitalism and capitalists. The working class could do it better and certainly to the benefit of working people. Why should millions starve, cope with unemployment, be sweated for subsist-

---

* Wars of independence in colonies and nominal ex-colonies were endemic, where national and socialist aspirations intertwined. This essay is not a general history. It omits analysis of Cuban and Vietnamese liberation and the establishment of socialism in eastern Europe after World War Two.

ence wages, and work in unsafe, unhealthy and just plain inhuman places while capitalists and their hangers-on squandered wealth on luxury consumption, periodically made a mess of the economy, and sent boys to die for plunder?

Socialism motivates committed persons in the class struggle at hand. It does so especially when they understand that socialism is not an ideal that happens to be preferable to other dreams. Rather, it is the only way to overcome the contradictions of the economic order. However, during the industrial era proper, the typical statement of socialism had less historical depth and immediacy than when Russian and Chinese revolutionaries had to solve urgent problems of revolution.

❖

The *Communist Manifesto* had stated the basic point: socialism is the "abolition of private property."[176] Private property is understood as factories and other means of production, not the clothes in your closet. The Communist Party of the Soviet Union in the 1930s gave a definition of "socialism, that is, the common ownership of the means of production and the distribution of products according to the work performed by each."[177] Usually such a definition specifies public ownership; the Soviet definition probably said common ownership in order to encompass full public ownership of factories and also the collective farms, which their members owned, not the Soviet people as a whole.

The clause about distribution of products left open the question of how to measure an individual's work. Workers in the Soviet Union did not all earn the same amount per hour, per ton of coal, per yard of cotton cloth.

Skilled work received a premium, and outstanding productiveness received a bonus. After the early 1930s, members of the Communist Party could receive above-average income. There was no capitalist income, neither dividends, nor shares and real property traded for capital gains, nor loaning of money for interest.*

The public ownership definition of socialism tends to bury historical motion. Capitalism is clearly a horrendous economic order for working people, but has it reached an impassible barrier to overall progress for the masses? An ahistorical concept was understandable when socialism was far away or emerged as a real possibility only in brief moments of extreme social stress. Compare Russia. In the two decades before 1917, socialists there hammered out the basic change to be achieved, both completion of the revolutionary agenda for the peasants and the job of socialist industrialization. The historical sense is obviously deeper.

Because the Soviet Union provided an outstanding contrast to capitalism during the great depression of the 1930s, there was a tendency to identify socialism with public ownership *and* highly administrative operation of the economy. Soviet plans allocated raw materials, specified the output of each factory and production site, balanced intermediate products with planned inputs to other factories and mills, and decided the major investment projects. The method worked during the first stages of indus-

---

* One sign of the trend away from socialist economy after 1956 was the gradual but persistent growth of deals between firms that were kept off the books, including illegal debt transactions and diversion of factory output from its planned destinations to commercial channels.

175

trialization, whatever its defects and whatever improvisations were required. In 1928, the year of the first five-year plan, the economy stood at approximately the same level as at the beginning of World War One. The Soviet people made their country a major industrial power by 1941.

The Nazis were stunned in World War Two when the country did not collapse from a single massive "blitzkrieg." The Soviet Union fought and won World War Two with divisions of tanks superior to Nazi Panzers, with massive artillery, and a defensive air force. The country fought the war at the prevailing global industrial level. Most important, the Soviet people would not give up their country to barbarism.*

Administrative plans were a practical success at basic industrialization. Adherents of so-called market socialism reject them in favor of a variety of schemes that dream of combining capitalism and socialism. They propose that profit results determine where to invest nominally public funds. Or they keep a strong connection between the profit of a firm and the income of the managers and perhaps a layer of the employees. They may try to make everyone a capitalist by "socializing" stock ownership and dispersing shares to all individuals.

No one is against all markets. Socialism does not allocate workers their socks; they buy the ones they like (although important items like meat that are still scarce may be rationed). It is even possible to have carefully operated markets in production equipment like machine tools and intermediate products like bulk plastic. The problem is a

---

* Partisan guerillas fought behind Nazi lines as an important supplement.

set of economic institutions which generate profit that has a private aspect. Market socialists would allow these, and then they attempt to tax the profit, regulate it, or disperse it widely after the fact. These schemes do not work. Where there is profit, there are its beneficiaries, dedicated to expanding the scope of economic activity that allows profit. There is exploitation of labor and accumulation of capital.

Examples of actual market socialism are rare. An early one was Yugoslavia after World War Two. Firms were organized as so-called workers' collectives, and the economy became enmeshed in capitalism. A larger, more recent example is China, where officials around Deng Xiaoping dissolved socialism at a gradual but accelerating pace from 1978 on. Their "socialism with Chinese characteristics" is sometimes described as market socialism. In reality, the new ruling class is capitalist. Some of the class are private individuals, like Jack Ma, mogul of the online giant of commerce Alibaba. Others are government officials who help family members seize the wealth of public factories, land, and other assets. China has indeed achieved rapid industrialization, sweated out of tens of millions of men and young women driven from home to toil at construction sites and in sweatshop factories.

❖

What does socialism offer at the end of industrial capitalism? We cannot answer with a list of wishes: Replace production for profit by production for needs, and then we will eradicate poverty, maintain full employment, ensure good health care for all, make retirement secure, reduce school class size, extend college to all who want it, and do it all in a way that restores clean air and reverses global warming. How? The reply generally is that we have the wealth and the productive capacity, and we will do it with democratic planning.

Such vacuous enthusiasm is acceptable agitation at times, but useless for serious politics.

Compare the task at hand with the alternative of reforms. They are generally measures that we can imagine being taken with a reasonable expectation of the result. For example, by extending the tax on Social Security to incomes above the current ceiling of $117,000, we can increase retirement benefits in line with inflation, puncturing gloomy lies about the impending bankruptcy of the fund. We can impose a customs tax on imports made with cheap labor, nudging U.S. corporations to locate production here. We can staff federal and state labor relations agencies with people empowered to take swift action when employers fire employees who talk union.

In place of reforms that propose a definite change in a law, policy, or agency, socialists advocate change that heralds a new life. A detailed blueprint is not required. In order to show people the essence of the new world, we need basic principles. People need to see in their mind's eye an economic order that can take the place of capitalism.

Socialist principles emerge from understanding of the historical problem. We began with the question, why did mass prosperity turn into endless decline around 1973? We found that capitalism could not move beyond standard labor. Three related principles of socialism today respond to the impasse of capitalist accumulation:

• We will move to a common prosperity wage for all.

• We will change corporations run for profit into firms chartered to break even.

• We will guarantee full employment.

Wages will narrow every year. A maximum wage, outlawing the gluttonous millions of dollars per year paid to corporate executives, can be set at once and reduced further over time. The minimum wage will rise on a schedule set out five or ten years in advance. The minimum will head toward a common prosperity wage for every worker. Socialism can do this; capitalist regimes go through a big battle just to raise the minimum wage a few dimes.

A recalculation of wages for the U.S. in 2007 (before the great depression) showed the economy capable of paying an equal wage of $72,394 while doubling Social Security retirement benefits.[178] Wages might be structured at $52,000 in one's first year of work, increasing a thousand dollars for each year of employment to a ceiling of $92,000 after 40 years. The exact schedule is not the point, so long as it applies to everyone.

The existing wage spread narrows over time as people become qualified for economically viable higher wages. When the regime schedules a narrowing of wage differences from year to year, firms know where wage costs will go. The government knows that workers must be more qualified in order to earn higher wages.

There should be no confusion between the no rich, no poor program and redistribution by taxing high incomes and aiding the poor. Every job exists because someone is needed to do the work. Humanity now has such resources and productive powers that our common responsibility is to qualify everyone for good work. As the minimum wage rises, we can automate more labor as well as raise the

179

content of what people do. We can work to satisfy advanced needs and to care for the earth that sustains us.

The operation of firms at breakeven is the way to abolish capital income. Society collects the surplus within production, not after the fact on realized profit. This can be done, for example, by a tax on each hour of employed labor.

Full employment is the easiest of the three principles to implement, done with public expenditure of the socialized surplus. Keynesian policies to this end have been known for decades. The only problem, which Keynesians ignore, is that capital does not play its assigned role. It refuses to invest and produce beyond the point of maximum profit. When we replace corporations with firms operated to break even, it becomes possible to balance economic activity to the point of full employment of all workers, which becomes their constitutional right.

There is a rutted road of arguments about whether we must reward some people with fabulous riches in order to have a dynamic society. Debate about "human nature" is not helpful. In a society of no rich and no poor, good work earns what most good workers want: an opportunity to choose the next job that is more important or more interesting, a desired occupation, perhaps a job in a different location. Even early retirement might be an item on the list. This method of individual reward, the proof of experience that better socialism means a better life, and the honor of society will call forth dedicated, energetic projects and their champions in every sphere of life.

In the early days there will be maniacs left over from capitalism who still want to acquire riches and to exert power by acquiring wealth or connections rather than by earning social admiration. They will indeed be frustrated.

Later, such types will disappear. How often these days do we see a fierce Viking warrior walking down the street? Each successive mode of life produces its characteristic spectrum of personalities.[179]

❖

A revolutionary regime could easily put into effect the three principles of no rich and no poor. They are definite actions, not a grab-bag description of what we would like. A typical example of the latter is in the founding constitution of Left Unity, a party formed in Britain in November 2013. The document is one of many that could be cited as evidence of the unfinished task of our time, which is to find and rally around a programmatic statement of socialism. No criticism unique to the British group is intended.

The Left Unity constitution states that the group aims "to win a mandate to govern and introduce radical and fundamental changes in British society based on our belief in the benefits of cooperation and community ownership instead of the chaotic competition of capitalism; universal human rights, internationalism and peace; social, political and economic equality for all in the fullest sense, without which true democracy and mutual respect cannot flourish; a democratically planned economy that is environmentally sustainable, within which all enterprises, whether privately owned, cooperatives or under public ownership operate in ways that promote the needs of the people and wider society; an inclusive welfare state which operates on the principle that each will contribute to society according to their ability to do so, and society will in return meet their needs."[180]

181

These are nice sentiments. Actually, the constitution does not use the word socialism; the paragraph quoted is the closest statement of an idea of it. At its founding convention Left Unity also adopted a bolder statement:

"We are *socialist* because our aim is to end capitalism. We will pursue a society where the meeting of human needs is paramount, not one which is driven by the quest for private profit and the enrichment of a few. The natural wealth, and the means of production, distribution and exchange will be owned in common and democratically run by and for the people as a whole, rather than being owned and controlled by a small minority to enrich themselves."[181]

Without doubt the aim of socialists is to put an end to capitalism. Still, the paragraph conveys no principles of economic operation. Making human needs is paramount is a noble but empty sentiment. The statement leaves too much to the clause that the people as a whole will operate the means of production "democratically." The reader might feel the sincerity of the statement's authors, but why would such vague praise of socialism impress her?

Parallel statements immediately follow declaring that the group is feminist, environmentalist, opposed to all forms of discrimination, and supports strong trade unions. These paragraphs are stronger and more convincing than the one about socialism. It is a weak socialist who cannot give genuine primacy to the relations of production, be definite about them, and put forward specific new principles that anyone can understand.

Left Unity does not say it a revolutionary organization. Its main activity will apparently be to participate in elections. It sets aside the question whether socialism can be achieved solely through such means as elections, demonstrations, and civil disobedience. A socialist could insist that it is a good idea to work in Left Unity, but she cannot point to much socialist content in its goals and program.

The International Socialist Organization is not a broad group devoted mainly to participating in elections like Left Unity. ISO aims to "unite the most radical elements."* Its statement of basic outlook, *Where We Stand*, invites the reader to: "Imagine a society where the means of production are held in common, by free association, and where labor is expended and allocated according to a social plan. Instead of things being produced only if they can be sold profitably, they are produced because they are socially necessary, and their production and distribution is carried out according to a democratically worked-out plan... That society is socialism."[182] ISO still relies on the static concept of public ownership and planning from the industrial era.

Left Unity, ISO and other declared adherents update socialism in one aspect; they add a phrase about a democratically worked-out plan. Few notions are cloudier. There are more ideas of democracy than there are varieties of roses, but the reader gets no idea of its basic content from ISO. "We'll be democratic" is an evasion of the duty to set forth a definite idea of socialist economy in motion.

❖

People join a revolution for different reasons. Many, perhaps most, decide they cannot take it any longer. They might still have something to lose, but obtaining what they

---

* There are indeed committed radicals in ISO. Criticism of the doctrine is the topic here.

need has become unbearable. They revolt against economic, social, and political oppression. "We, who were nothing, shall be all!"[183]

Other people get by in the existing order and may even be comfortable, but they are frustrated that a world of possibilities is blocked. These persons see that they could build, produce, discover and develop new material wonders, create new culture, and organize new institutions that promote rather than hinder social progress. "A better world's in birth!"[184]

An important characteristic of bourgeois revolutions was these two motivations tended to diverge according to class. Those who would accept exploitation no longer and fought the existing exploiters were generally the peasants or farmers, poorer craftsmen, and small shopowners, while those driven to build new kinds of wealth were members of and aspirants to the new exploiting class. In the English revolution of the 1640s, the latter were better-off farmers and some business owners.

The early revolutions were waged on religious-political grounds. The real content was a transformed state that enforced new economic principles. Freeing land and commerce from the parasitic exactions of lords, the monarch, and the church meant that property could function as capital, bringing riches to its owner. Meanwhile, small farmers were squeezed off the land and reduced to tenants and wage workers. Their labor created the new landed and manufactory capitalist wealth.

In the French Revolution of 1789, the vision was more openly economic than it had been in old England. The full title of the famous *Encyclopédie* of the pre-revolutionary Enlightenment, pushed to completion by Denis Diderot, was the Encyclopedia, or a Systematic Dictionary of Science, Arts, and the Trades. Actually, most of the articles documented practical arts and craft knowledge that post-revolutionary industrial technology would soon render obsolete. No matter. The Encyclopedia inspired close engagement with the material world to make new, useful things and become wealthy thereby.

In France, many of the bourgeois ideologists and activists were lawyers, journalists, and provincial functionaries. This was one stream of the Revolution. Another was the peasant masses, whom the nobility and the state believed to be eternally submissive, apart from an occasional local rebellion. The peasants unleashed an unstoppable flood of fury, determined to sweep aside the aristocracy and escape gaunt lives in the midst of rich harvests.

The early bourgeoisies embodied the bittersweet character of the revolutions that overthrew an agrarian economic order. They fought to advance productive powers, creating potentially better conditions for all; then they replaced agrarian rent, dues, and taxes with the exploitation of wage labor.

This ambiguity disappears in the revolution that approaches us. Completing industrialization, capitalist society confronts an irresolvable contradiction of accumulation. The discontent of the masses swells just as it did in agrarian England and France, tsarist Russia and dynastic China. In addition, the unstoppable drive toward a new stage of production and labor, which formerly resided in a nascent bourgeoisie, now stirs within the working class.

People who wring their hands over the lack of revolutionary agents today (such as the near-disappearance of large, cohesive ranks of factory workers in core industries) may reflect on both the direction and creative variety of history. The masses do move; they are not eternally quiescent. The most committed revolutionaries are those who, when the crucial moment arrives, have already adopted the vision of the new society in their heart and mind.

Socialist society takes on the great project of no rich and no poor, of expanding material equality and prosperity, unlocking and developing the talents of all. The revolutionaries of three and four hundred years ago could not foresee how humanity would engage with the material world. Today, we, too, know only abstractly that the people of a liberated economic order will bring forth new wonders from the world around us, to be enjoyed by everyone, with responsibility to future generations, both unleashing and respecting nature from which all blessings flow.

Tables

Table 1. Occupation of Employed Civilian U.S. Workers, 1950, 1970, and 2000

1950	Pct.	1970	Pct.	2000	Pct.
Professional, technical, and kindred	9.0%	Professional, technical, and kindred	14.8%	Professional and related	20.2%
Farmers and farm managers	8.1%	Farmers and farm managers	2.1%	Farming, fishing, and forestry	0.7%
Managers, officials, and proprietors, excluding farm	9.1%	Managers and administrators, except farm	8.3%	Management, business, and financial operations	13.5%
Clerical and kindred workers	12.3%	Clerical and kindred workers	17.9%	Office and administrative support	15.4%
Sales workers	6.8%	Sales workers	7.1%	Sales and related	11.2%
Craftsmen, foremen, and kindred workers	13.9%	Craftsmen and kindred workers	13.8%	Construction, extraction, and maintenance	9.4%
Operatives and kindred workers	20.1%	Operatives, except transport	13.7%	Production occupations	8.5%
		Transport equipment operatives	0	Transportation and material moving	0
Private household workers	2.6%	Private household workers	1.5%		
Service workers, except private household	7.5%	Service workers, except private household	11.2%	Service occupations	14.9%
Farmer laborers, except unpaid, and foremen	2.8%	Farm laborers and farm foremen	1.2%		
Farm laborers, unpaid family workers	1.7%				
Laborers, except farm and mine	6.1%	Laborers, except farm	4.6%		
Total	100.0%	Total	100.0%	Total	100.0%

U.S. Census 1952, Table 221; U.S. Census 1970, Table 223; U.S. Census 2000 Summary File 3, Table QT-P27.

Table 2. Employment in manufacturing and selected industries (000s)

	1950			1960		
	Total employed	Production workers	Pct prod.	Total employed	Production workers	Pct prod.
Total manufacturing	15,241	12,523	82.2%	16,762	12,562	74.9%
Selected industries:						
Transportation equipment except motor vehicles	449	352	78.4%	889	566	63.7%
Electrical equipment and supplies	991	770	77.7%	1,446	987	68.3%
Instruments and related products	250	189	75.6%	354	232	65.5%
Chemicals and allied products	640	461	72.0%	830	511	61.6%
Printing, publishing, and allied industries	748	494	66.0%	917	592	64.6%
Paper and allied products	485	416	85.8%	593	474	79.9%
Machinery (except electrical)	1,210	929	76.8%	1,471	1,030	70.0%
Fabricated metal products	982	812	82.7%	1,129	869	77.0%
Furniture and fixtures	364	317	87.1%	383	319	83.3%
Apparel and related products	1,202	1,080	89.9%	1,228	1,004	81.8%
Food and kindred products	1,790	1,331	74.4%	1,793	1,211	67.5%
Primary metal industries	1,247	1,075	86.2%	1,229	992	80.7%
Motor vehicles and equipment	816	677	83.0%	728	567	77.9%
Lumber and wood products (excl. furniture)	808	745	92.2%	637	570	89.5%
Textile mill products	1,256	1,169	93.1%	915	827	90.4%
Selected industries as percent of all mfg.	86.9%	86.4%		86.8%	85.6%	

Selected industries are sorted by rate of job growth, 1950 to 1960.
Fabricated metal excludes machinery, trans. equip., and ordnance.
Table 291, Statistical Abstract of the U.S., 1962.

Table 3. Investment in private nonresidential equipment and software

Investment in private nonresidential equipment and software	1950	1960	1970	1980	1990	2000	2010
Information processing equipment	10%	16%	21%	26%	32%	31%	27%
Software	0%	0%	3%	4%	12%	20%	27%
Industrial and other equipment	54%	56%	53%	50%	42%	32%	34%
Transportation equipment	36%	27%	22%	20%	15%	17%	12%
Total	100%	100%	100%	100%	100%	100%	100%

U.S. Bur. of Econ Analysis, Table 2.7. Investment in Private Fixed Assets, Equipment and Software, and Structures by Type.

Notes

This book benefitted greatly from review and comments. I am grateful for crucial help from Raj Sahai, Greg Godels, Allan Miller and anonymous reviewers.

1 According to the National Bureau of Economic Research, the peak before it began was December 2007. We will call it the depression of 2008. NBER, "US Business Cycle Expansions and Contractions" at http://www.nber.org/cycles/cyclesmain.html.

2 U.S. Bureau of Labor Statistics, Labor Force Statistics from the Current Population Survey, not seasonally adjusted, civilian labor force 16 years and over at http://www.bls.gov/data/.

3 U.S. Dept. of Agriculture, Supplemental Nutrition Assistance Program Participation and Costs, average participation per year, at http://www.fns.usda.gov/pd/SNAPsummary.htm.

4 U.S. Bur. of Labor Statistics, Employment, Hours, and Earnings from the Current Employment Statistics survey (National) and Consumer Price Index - All Urban Consumers, calculated from number employed, average hours of work per week, and average hourly wage, not seasonally adjusted at http://www.bls.gov/data/.

5 Arthur C. Brooks, "Making a moral case for capitalism," *Philadelphia Inquirer*, October 21, 2012. Brooks is president of the American Enterprise Institute and author of *The Road to Freedom*. A liberal economist, Thomas Piketty, idolizes the capitalist entrepreneur, too. His popular *Capital in the Twenty-First Century* worries only about rentier capitalists who enjoy huge incomes from bond interest, stock dividends, etc.

6 U.S. Govt. Printing Office, *Economic Report of the President 2008*, Table B-47.

7 Philip L. Rones et al, "Trends in hours of work since the mid-1970s," U.S. Bur. of Labor Statistics, *Monthly Labor Review*, April 1997, Table 3 and U.S. Census Bureau, *Statistical Ab-*

stract 2008, Table 582. In addition, some workers hold two part-time jobs.

[8] U.S. Census Bureau, Employment and population data from the Current Population Survey, not seasonally adjusted, age 20 and over.

[9] Workers' share computed as the number of workers multiplied by their average earnings at the median. Use of the median in effect excludes some people who are paid huge salaries that account for the gap of average earnings over median earnings per worker. U.S. Bur. of the Census, Weekly and Hourly Earnings, Current Population Survey, unadjusted, 16 years and over at http://www.bls.gov/data/#wages. GDP from U.S. Bur. of Economic Analysis, Table 1.1.5 at http://www.bea.gov. The data series is reported from 1979. The *average* weekly earnings of private-sector employees, in constant dollars, were 14 percent less in 2011 than the high point reached in 1973. U.S. Govt. Printing Office, *Economic Report of the President 2012*, Table B-47.

[10] Federal Reserve Bank of New York, "Quarterly Report on Household Debt and Credit," Feb. 2014, data sheet.

[11] David A. Mindell, "Automation's Finest Hour: Radar and System Integration in World War II," in Thomas P. Hughes and Agatha Hughes, eds., *Systems, Experts, and Computers: The Systems Approach in Management and Engineering, World War II and After*, Cambridge, MA, MIT Press, p. 47.

[12] "[Vannevar] Bush's Analog Solution," Computer History Museum at http://www.computerhistory.org/revolution/analog-computers/3/143.

[13] Norbert Wiener, *The Human Use of Human Beings*, New York, Da Capo, 1954, p. 162.

[14] Result on "automation," case insensitive, from Google Ngram Viewer at http://books.google.com/ngrams/.

[15] Ben B. Seligman, *Most Notorious Victory: Man in an Age of Automation*, Glencoe, IL, Free Press, 1966, p. 118.

[16] Ibid., p. 128.

[17] Ibid., p. 130.

[18] Walter S. Buckingham, Jr., "Industrial Significance," in Joseph C. O'Mahoney et al, *The Challenge of Automation: Papers Delivered at the National Conference on Automation*, Washington, D.C., Public Affairs Press, 1955, p. 41.

[19] Seligman, op. cit., p. 131.

[20] Ibid., p. 132.

[21] Ibid., p. 155.

[22] Ibid., p. 118.

[23] Ibid., p. 117.

[24] Stephen Meyer, "An Economic 'Frankenstein': UAW Workers' Response to Automation at the Ford Brook Park Plant in the 1950s," *Michigan Historical Review*, v. 28, 2002 at http://www.autolife.umd.umich.edu/Labor/L_Casestudy/L_Casestudy.htm.

[25] Ben Seligman, "Data on Automation," memo to Victor Reuther, April 17, 1957, p. 1f., quoted in Donald R. Stabile, "Automation, workers and union decline: Ben Seligman's contribution to the institutional economics of labor," *Labor History*, Vol. 49, No. 3, August 2008, p. 282.

[26] Walter P. Reuther, "Labor's Stake," in Joseph C. O'Mahoney, op. cit., p. 51.

[27] Industrial Union Dept., AFL-CIO, Automation and Major Technological Change: Collective Bargaining Problems, Washington, D.C., 1958, p. 8f.

[28] Robert Heilbroner, Foreword, in Seligman, *Most Notorious Victory*, p. ix.

[29] "Statics and Dynamics in Economics," *International Encyclopedia of the Social Sciences*, 1968, reproduced at http://www.encyclopedia.com/doc/1G2-3045001199.html.

[30] Woodrow Wilson, Address to The New York City High School Teachers Association, Jan. 9th, 1909, at www.johntaylorgatto.com/fourthpurpose/ short.htm.

[31] Karl Marx and Frederick Engels, *Manifesto of the Communist Party*, ch. 1, Beijing, Foreign Languages Press, 1968, p. 34f.

[32] National Science Board, *Science and Engineering Indicators 2010*, Arlington, National Science Foundation, 2010, p. 3-11; *Statistical Abstract 1952*, Table 207.

[33] Walter S. Buckingham, Jr., op cit., p. 32.

[34] Dirk Struik, *Origins of American Science*, New York, Cameron, p. 169f.

[35] Georg Lukács, *The Ontology of Social Being: 3. Labour*, London, Merlin Press, 1980, p. 61f. The manuscript was not published in his lifetime.

[36] Statistical Abstract 1962, Tables 777 and 779.

[37] While freight railroad business was stagnant, trucks and pipelines carried more goods. Trucks benefitted from the federal freeway construction program launched under President Eisenhower.

[38] Statistical Abstract 1974, Table 964.

[39] W. David Kingery, "The Transition Of Ceramics From Craft To Science-Based Industry," 13th World Congress on Ceramic Tile Quality, p. 15 at http://www.qualicer.org/recopilatorio/ponencias/pdf/9811010e.pdf

[40] More at http://www.apawood.org/level_b.cfm?content=srv_med_new_bkgd_plycen.

[41] IEEE, "Women and Electrical and Electronics Manufacturing," at http://www.ieeeghn.org/wiki/index.php/Women_and_Electrical_and_Electronics_Manufacturing.

[42] Reproduced by Tom J. Sawyer at http://tjsawyer.com/B205solder.php.

[43] James B. Carey in Joseph C. O'Mahoney et al, op cit., p. 65.

[44] History of Titanium Dioxide Whites at http://www.webexhibits.org/pigments/indiv/history/tiwhite.html.

[45] D. A. Buckingham et al, *Titanium Sponge Statistics*, U.S. Geological Survey, 2012 at http://minerals.usgs.gov/ds/2005/140/ds140-timet.pdf.

Notes

[46] Vannevar Bush, Office of Scientific Research and Development, *Science: The Endless Frontier*, U.S. Govt. Printing Office, 1945, pp. 14, 3.

[47] John Markoff, "Skilled Work, Without the Worker," *New York Times*, August 18, 2012.

[48] *China Daily*, Nov. 14, 2013. The labor cost figure presumably includes benefits.

[49] C. Custer, "Why China's about to get a lot more robots," TechInAsia.com, October 9, 2014 at http://www.techinasia.com/decade-china-buy-ton-robots/.

[50] National Science Board, op. cit., Fig. 3-1, p. 3-13.

51 Roni Caryn Rabin and Kaiser Health News, "A growing number of primary-care doctors are burning out," *Washington Post*, March 31, 2014.

[52] Megan M. Barker, "Manufacturing employment hard hit during the 2007–09 recession," *Monthly Labor Review*, U.S. Bur. of Labor Statistics, April 2011, p. 28; *Statistical Abstract 1962*, Table 291.

[53] U.S. Bur. of Labor Statistics, *Handbook of Methods*, ch. 2 at http://www.bls.gov/opub/hom/homch2.htm#concepts.

[54] Wyndham Mortimer, *Organize!: My Life as a Union Man*, Beacon Press, 1971, p. 195.

[55] Ibid., p. 196. Mortimer entangled his insight with "the flight of our boasted technology to other highly developed industrial nations."

[56] Joe Allen, "Taking sides on Harrington," Socialist Worker website, May 8, 2013, http://socialistworker.org/2013/05/08/taking-sides-on-harrington.

[57] "Charlie Rose Talks to Bridgewater's Ray Dalio," *Business Week*, Feb. 10, 2014.

[58] Commission on the Skills of the American Workforce, *America's Choice: high skills or low wages!*, Rochester, National Center on Education and the Economy, 1990, pp. 1, 2.

[59] Ibid., p. 3.

[60] Ibid., p. 2.

[61] Result on "financialization," case insensitive, from Google Ngram Viewer at http://books.google.com/ngrams/.

[62] Lawrence H. Summers, Treasury Deputy Secretary Lawrence H. Summers Testimony Before The Senate Committee On Agriculture, Nutrition, And Forestry On The CFTC Concept Release, U.S. Treasury Dept., July 30, 1998, at http://www.treasury.gov/press-center/press-releases/Pages/rr2616.asp.

[63] William D. Cohan, "Rethinking Robert Rubin," *Business Week*, Sept. 30, 2012.

[64] Matt Palmquist, "The Auto Industry's Big Bailout Bounce," July 26, 2013 at http://www.strategy-business.com/article/re00245; Jon Cassidy, "Ohio workers protest Biden, 'dark side of auto bailout'," *Ohio Watchdog*, September 12, 2012 at http://watchdog.org/56061/oh-delphi-protesters-expected-at-biden-speech/.

[65] Federal Reserve Bank, Corporate Equities issues at http://www.federalreserve.gov/releases/z1/Current/data.htm.

[66] Federal Reserve System, Table D.3. Credit Market Debt Outstanding by Sector, Federal Reserve Statistical Release Z.1, Financial Accounts of the United States using domestic nonfinancial sectors, credit market instruments, liability at http://www.federalreserve.gov/releases/Z1/default.htm. GDP from U.S. Bur. of Economic Analysis, Table 1.1.5 at http://www.bea.gov.

[67] Ibid. Nonfinancial corporations' financial income from Greta R. Krippner, "The financialization of the American economy," Socio-*Economic Review*, 2005, 3, p. 185.

[68] Krippner, op. cit. p. 179.

[69] "Volcker Asserts U.S Must Trim Living Standard," Oct. 18, 1979, p. 1.

[70] U.S. Dept. of Labor, *Private Pension Plan Bulletin Historical Tables and* Graphs, 2010 Data Rel. 1.0, Nov. 2012, Table E8 at http://www.dol.gov/ebsa/pdf/historicaltables.pdf.

Notes

[71] Matthew P. Fink, *The Rise of Mutual Funds: An Insider's View*, Oxford University Press, 2nd ed., 2011, p. 118.

[72] U.S. Dept. of Labor, Employee Benefits Security Admin., *Private Pension Plan Bulletin Historical Tables and Graphs*, June 2013, Table E8 at http://www.dol.gov/ebsa/pdf /historicaltables.pdf.

[73] Ibid., Table E11.

[74] Federal Reserve System, *Flow of Funds Accounts of the United States*, Table L.100 Households and Nonprofit Organizations at http://www.federalreserve.gov/releases/z1/Current/data.htm.

[75] Christopher Chase-Dunn et al, "Trade Globalization Since 1795: Waves of Integration in the World-System," *American Sociological Review*, Feb. 2000, Fig. 3. Their index of the openness of trade computes the ratio of imports to GDP in each country, then calculates a global average weighting each country by population. This method eliminates difficulties that mar trade statistics computed with currency adjustments.

[76] William H. Branson, Herbert Giersch, and Peter G. Peterson, "Trends in United States International Trade and Investment since World War II," Table 3.8, in Martin Feldstein, ed., *The American Economy in Transition*, Univ. of Chicago Press, 1980, p. 191.

[77] Peter Temin, "The Golden Age of European growth reconsidered," *European Review of Economic History*, 6, Cambridge Univ. Press, 2002, p. 4.

[78] Bruce Western and Kieran Healy, "Explaining the OECD Wage Slowdown: Recession or Labour Decline?", *European Sociology Review*, 15:3, 1999, p. 234.

[79] For example, Ismael Hossein-Zadeh, "Keynes is Dead; Long Live Marx!: The Death Grip of Neoliberalism," CounterPunch, August 26, 2014 at http://www.counterpunch.org/2014/08 /26/keynes-is-dead-long-live-marx/. He argues that globalized struggle between advanced capitals led them to neoliberal policies, which are for him the substance of the worsened condition of workers since 1973.

80 For an example of this error worked out at length, see Robert Brenner, *The Economics of Global Turbulence*, Verso, London, 2006. When, for example, German and Japanese firms invaded U.S. markets, he asserts "an over-supply of manufacturing capacity and output resulting in downward pressure on product prices that lowered the rate of return on capital stock." (p. 142) For Brenner, profit consists of monopoly or oligopoly profit derived from prices held above costs. His outlook "takes as its starting point the anarchy and competitiveness of capitalist production" – and it forever chases interactions of individual capitals with no awareness of the general rate of profit. Narrative poses as explanation. (p. xx)

81 Robert E. Scott, *The Wal-Mart Effect*, Washington, D.C., Economic Policy Institute, June 25, 2007, p. 2 at http://s2.epi .org/page/-/old/issuebriefs/235/ib235.pdf.

82 U.S. Bur. of Economic Analysis, Table 4.2.5. Exports and Imports of Goods and Services by Type of Product at http: //www.bea.gov/iTable/index_nipa.cfm. Exports are nonagricultural goods; imports are goods except petroleum.

83 U.S. Bur. of Economic Analysis, GDPbyInd_VA_NAICS_1998-2011.xls.

84 U.S. Bur. of Economic Analysis, Table 12. U.S. International Transactions by Area. Gross imports of goods were one percent of U.S. GDP.

85 Wayne M. Morrison, *China-U.S. Trade Issues*, Congressional Research Service, May 21, 2012, Table 1 at http://www.fas.org /sgp/crs/row/RL33536.pdf. Datum is for 2011.

86 William Hinton, *The Great Reversal: The Privatization of China*, New York, 1990, pp. 180-82. Hinton was an eyewitness.

87 Interfax, "About 60 percent of Russians see communism as good system – poll," October 12, 2013 at http://rbth.ru/news /2013/10/12/about_60_percent_of_russians_see_communism _as_good_system_-_poll_30755.html.

Notes

88 Marx's schema of expanded reproduction (*Capital*, v. 2, ch. XXI, New York, International Publishers, 1967) is thus excluded, but the economy develops; it is not simple reproduction.

89 The socialist but non-Marxist economist Michal Kalecki ignores the phase condition. He believes that prosperity is limited only because "under a regime of permanent full employment, the 'sack' would cease to play its role as a disciplinary measure. ... Strikes for wage increases and improvements in conditions of work would create political tension. It is true that profits would be higher under a regime of full employment than they are on the average under laissez-faire; and even the rise in wage rates resulting from the stronger bargaining power of the workers is less likely to reduce profits than to increase prices, and thus adversely affects only the rentier interests. But 'discipline in the factories' and 'political stability' are more appreciated than profits by business leaders." The description of capitalist antagonism to wage increases is certainly accurate. There is an inevitable gap between full employment and capitalist full employment. However, Kalecki rejects the fact that capitalist prosperity contains a contradiction and must come to an end. He entertains the economic feasibility of capitalism without slumps because he does not use the labor theory of value. Kalecki, "Political Aspects of Full Employment", *Political Quarterly*, vol. 14, no. 3, Oct. 1943, p. 326.

90 In labor theory of value, $r = s / (C + V)$. The general rate of profit is r. The annual flow of profit in the broadest sense is s. The stock of capital value is C. The stock of value for wages, V, is fairly small; the short time of production of most wage goods means that while the flow v is significant for the year, the stock on hand at any time does not need to be large. The governing change in this equation is the relentless rise of C during prosperity. An exposition of the basic concepts and propositions of the labor theory of value is in chapters two to five of my *From Capitalism to Equality*.

[91] Transcript of Larry Summers speech at the IMF Economic Forum, Nov. 8, 2013 at http://m.facebook.com/notes/randy-fellmy/transcript-of-larry-summers-speech-at-the-imf-economic-forum-nov-8-2013/585630634864563.

[92] U.S. Office of Technology Assessment, *Computerized Manufacturing Automation: Employment, Education, and the Workplace*, April 1984, pp. 5, 7.

[93] Charles Andrews, *No Rich, No Poor*, Oakland, Needle Press, p. 74f.

[94] John C. Gallawa, *The Complete Microwave Oven Service Handbook*, 2000 at http://illumin.usc.edu/76/the-engineering-behind-the-microwave-oven/ Also, "These manufacturers also have relatively large expenditures for research and development of new magnetron types and processing. Most of the assembly lines that make consumer-type magnetrons are completely automated." Wayne Love, "Magnetrons," in T. Koryu Ishii, *Handbook of Microwave Technology*, Vol. 2, San Diego, Academic Press, 1995, p. 34.

[95] U.S. Bur. of Economic Analysis, Table 2.7. Investment in Private Fixed Assets, Equipment and Software, and Structures by Type.

[96] Jon Faust, "Judging Investment Strength: Taking Account of High Tech," *Economic Review*, Federal Reserve Bank of Kansas City, Nov-Dec. 1990, p. 10. A piece of equipment may pass through several owners that conduct different businesses before it is melted down or thrown away.

[97] David Nasaw, *Andrew Carnegie*, New York, Penguin, 2006, p. 181.

[98] "Iron and Steel Industry," *Encyclopaedia Britannica*, volume 12, 1972 edition, p. 611.

[99] *Iron Trade Review*, March 30, 1911, p. 625.

[100] Thomas J. Misa, *A Nation of Steel*, Baltimore, Johns Hopkins University Press, 1995, p. 83.

[101] Much of the innovation is first conceived then guided and financed by the federal government. Mariana Mazzucato, *The*

Notes

Entrepreneurial State: Debunking Public vs. Private Sector Myths, London, Anthem, 2013. One of the first important chip firms, Fairchild Semiconductor, depended on federal contracts and military product requirements in its first years, which coincided with the post-Sputnik alarm over technological leadership. Chong-Moon Lee, *The Silicon Valley Edge*, Stanford Univ. Press, p. 159. As for research and considerable development leading up to product innovation, a Defense Department study found that in 1952 government paid for 60 percent of research and development but performed only 21 percent of it, while industry performed 68 percent of all R&D but paid for only 38 percent of it. (Blank and Stigler, Table 6, p. 14.) Businesses that do research should be divided into firms that carry out contracts by innovative federal agencies like the Defense Advanced Research Projects Agency and the National Institutes of Health, and corporations that fund research with their own capital.

[102] David Isenberg, Rise Of The Stupid Network, June 4, 1997 at http://www.isen.com.

[103] U.S. Bur. of Economic Analysis, Table 2.7. Investment in Private Fixed Assets, Equipment and Software, and Structures by Type.

[104] National Employment Law Project, *The Low-Wage Recovery and Growing Inequality*, August 2012, p. 2 at http://www.nelp.org/page/-/Job_Creation/LowWageRecovery2012.pdf.

[105] Ibid., p. 4.

[106] U.S. Bur. of Economic Analysis, Table 1.10. Gross Domestic Income by Type of Income.

[107] Ibid. The standard Pearson correlation formula was used.

[108] Andrew Kliman contends that the income of the working class as a percentage of GDI has not declined over the past thirty-five years. In defense of combining wage and supplemental compensation amounts, he asserts: "One needs to recognise that workers' receipt of income is one thing, while the exchange of that income for goods and services (bread, medical benefits) of

equivalent value is another thing. It also helps to think about what would happen if these medical benefits were taken away. Workers would be worse off, wouldn't they?." ("Underestimating Evidence, Capitalists and Workers: A Rejoinder to Sam Gindin," New Left Project, May 19, 2014 at http://www.newleftproject .org/index.php/site/article_comments/underestimating_eviden ce_capitalists_and_workers_a_rejoinder_to_sam_gindin.) Kliman builds his conclusion into the phrase about exchanging income for bread and medical benefits of "equivalent value" per income dollar. If bread and health care prices rose at about the same rate, we could reasonably add them together and compare them over the years. But they do not.

[109] Table B–29, Sources of personal income, 1964–2012, *Economic Report of the President 2013.*

[110] Congressional Budget Office, *The Distribution of Household Income and Federal Taxes, 2010*, Washington, Dec. 2013 at http://www.cbo.gov/publication/44604.

[111] Tables 126 and 121, Statistical Abstract 1953.

[112] Table 140, *Statistical Abstract*; Table 5.23.5, National Income Product Accounts, Bureau of Economic Analysis. The education figure is exaggerated by double counting, since it includes both capital outlays during the year and interest paid on past outlays. By surplus we mean here the resources available after consumption by all classes and after funding government services, from road maintenance to "defense."

[113] Richard Vedder et al, *Why Are Recent College Graduates Underemployed?: University Enrollments and Labor-Market Realities*, Washington, Center for College Affordability and Productivity, Jan. 2013, Fig. 1. The percentage is substantial even allowing for the authors' possibly subjective categorization of occupation to education.

[114] National Nurses United, "RNs Urge Tougher Federal Oversight on Unproven Medical Technology on which Hospitals Spend Billions," July 8, 2014 at http://www.nationalnursesunited.org

Notes

/press/entry/nurses-urge-tougher-federal-oversight-on-unproven-medical-technology-on-whi/.

[115] Diane Ravitch, "Why I Changed My Mind About School *Reform," Wall Street Journal*, March 9, 2010.

[116] Ki Mae Heussner, "Investment in K-12 education innovation is soaring, but it's not all rosy," Aug. 2, 2012 at http://gigaom .com/2012/08/02/investment-in-k-12-education-innovation-is-soaring-but-its-not-all-rosy/.

[117] Bill Gates, Remarks to National Charter Schools Conference, June 29, 2010. at http://www.gatesfoundation.org/media-center/speeches/2010/06/national-charter-schools-conference.

[118] Charles Andrews, "Concentration Of U.S. Hospitals 1991-1999 And Its Implications For A National Health Program," *Intl. J. of Health Services*, vol. 35, no. 1, 2005.

[119] Table 1.2, Medicare & Medicaid Statistical Supplement, Centers for Medicare & Medicaid Services, 2010 at http://www .cms.gov/Research-Statistics-Data-and-Systems/Research/MedicareMedicaidStatSupp/2010.html.

[120] Mark Ames, "How Silicon Valley's most celebrated CEOs conspired to drive down 100,000 tech engineers' wages," January 23, 2014 at http://pando.com/2014/01/23/the-techtopus-how-silicon-valleys-most-celebrated-ceos-conspired-to-drive-down-100000-tech-engineers-wages/; Jonathan Stempel, "Silicon Valley workers may pursue collusion case as group – court," Reuters, Jan 14, 2014.

[121] Arthur A. Bright, Jr., *The Electric-Lamp Industry: Technological Change and Economic Development from 1800 to 1947*, New York, Macmillan, 1949, p. 331.

[122] George W. Stocking and Myron W. Watkins, *Cartels in Action: Case Studies in International Business Diplomacy*, Twentieth Century Fund, New York, 1946, pp. 356, 355.

[123] Ibid., p. 359.

[124] Ibid., p. 354.

[125] Arthur Bright, op cit, p. 333n.

[126] F. M. Scherer, "Pricing, Profits, and Technological Progress in the Pharmaceutical Industry," *J. of Economic Perspectives*, Vol. 7, 1993, p. 98.

[127] History of Aspirin at http://www.aspree.org/AUS/aspree-content/aspirin/history-aspirin.aspx.

[128] U.S. Senate, *Examination of the Pharmaceutical Industry, 1973-74*, Part 3, p. 867, quoted in Peter Temin, *The Evolution of the Modern Pharmaceutical Industry*, Working paper 223, Dept. of Economics, Cambridge, Mass. Inst. of Technology, Sept. 1978, p. 3.

[129] National Vital Statistics System, National Center for Health Statistics, Centers for Disease Control at http://www.cdc.gov/nchs/products/life_tables.htm. The figures are for whites; the shortfall of Black life expectancy decreased over time but death still took them five years sooner in 2000.

[130] Temin, op cit, p. 14.

[131] American Chemical Society, "The Pharmaceutical Golden Era: 1930 - 60" at http://pubs.acs.org/cen/coverstory/83/8325/8325golden.html.

[132] Public Citizen, "Pharmaceuticals Rank as Most Profitable Industry, Again,", Washington, graph 4 at http://www.citizen.org/documents/fortune500_2002erport.PDF.

[133] Ibid., p. 5.

[134] U.S. General Accounting Office, Technology Transfer: NIH-Private Sector Partnership in the Development of Taxol, Washington, D.C., June 2003, p. 3f.

[135] National Science Foundation, *Science and Engineering Indicators 2014*, Appendix Table 4-38 at http://www.nsf.gov/statistics/seind14/index.cfm/chapter-4/c4h.htm.

[136] David H. Austin et al, *Research and Development in the Pharmaceutical Industry*, Washington, Congressional Budget Office, Oct. 2006, p. 3.

[137] National Science Foundation., op. cit., Appendix Table 4-31.

Notes

[138] U.S. Food and Drug Administration, "NDAs approved in calendar years 1990–2003 by therapeutic potentials and chemical types," Jan 21, 2004 quoted in Marcia Angell, "Over and Above: Excess in the pharmaceutical industry," *Canadian Medical Assoc. J.*, vol. 171, no. 12, Dec. 7, 2004, p. 1451.

[139] Angell, op. cit., p. 1451.

[140] Calculated from U.S. Census, "Drugs and Medicines," *Census of Manufactures*, vol. II, 1963 and 1967 editions and U.S. Census, *Current Industrial Reports*, 2006 -2010, Table 1.

[141] Alfred DuPont Chandler, *The Visible hand: The Managerial Revolution in American Business*, Cambridge, Harvard Univ. Press, 1977, p. 572.

[142] Moody's Investor Service, *Moody's Industrial Manual*, 1971, New York, pp. 598ff., 2014ff.; Securities and Exchange Comm., Form 10-K filings, 2011 and 2012.

[143] Auto Manufacturer Market Share in America: Oct. 2013 at www.GoodCarBadCar.net.

[144] Form 10-K, Securities and Exchange Comm., 2011, p. 6.

[145] Patrick McCray, Where Did That iPod Come From? at http://www.patrickmccray.com/2014/04/09/where-did-that-ipod-come-from/; Mariana Mazzucato, *The Entrepreneurial State: Debunking Public vs. Private Sector Myths*, London, Anthem, 2013, p. 97.

[146] Mazzucato, op. cit., p. 102.

[147] Ibid., p. 106.

[148] Yuqing Xing and Neal Detert, *How the iPhone Widens the United States Trade Deficit with the People's Republic of China*, Tokyo, Asian Development Bank Institute, Dec. 2010 quoting Andrew Rassweiler, "iPhone 3G S Carries $178.96 BOM and Manufacturing Cost, iSuppli Teardown Reveals," iSuppli, June 24, 2009 at http://www.isuppli.com/Teardowns -Manufacturing-and-Pricing/News/Pages/iPhone-3G-S-Carries-178-96-BOM-and-Manufacturing-Cost-iSuppli-Teardown-Reveals.aspx.

[149] Tim Culpan, "Apple Profit Margins Rise at Foxconn's Expense: Chart of the Day," Bloomberg News, Jan 4, 2012 at http://www.bloomberg.com/news/2012-01-04/apple-profit-margins-rise-at-foxconn-s-expense.html.

[150] Megan McArdle, "Why Can't Walmart Be More Like Costco?", *Daily Beast*, Nov 26, 2012 at http://www.thedailybeast.com /articles/2012/11/26/why-can-t-walmart-be-more-like-costco.html.

[151] Forms 10-K, Securities and Exchange Commission for fiscal year ended 8/31/2008 at Costco and 1/31/2008 at Walmart. Comparison shows approximately the same results in previous years.

[152] The I.W.W. believed it impossible that a unions could be both stable and militant to a revolutionary standard. Accordingly, I.W.W. unions rejected dues check-off, did not build up strike funds, and attempted to foreshadow the ideal of one big union by a rule that all union cards were universally transferable. Philip S. Foner, *History of the Labor Movement in the United States*, vol. 4, New York, International, 1965, p. 471.

[153] U.S. Bur. of Labor Statistics, Union Membership Data From The National Directory Series, Table A. Union members are the annual average number of dues paying members reported by labor unions. Data exclude members of professional and public employee associations.

[154] Al Hart, "Labor Should Fight for Single-Payer Retirement, Health Care," *Labor Notes*, May 27, 2007 at http://www .labornotes.org/2007/05/viewpoint-labor-should-fight-single-payer-retirement-health-care.

[155] Social realist unionists in the 1930s and 1940s were often members or friends of the Communist Party. For a study of their militancy and devotion to democracy within the union, see Judith Stepan-Norris and Maurice Zeitlin, *Left Out: Reds and America's Industrial Unions*, Cambridge, Cambridge Univ. Press, 2003.

[156] U.S. Bur. of Labor Statistics, op. cit.

Notes

[157] U.S. Bur. of Labor Statistics, Work Stoppage Data at http://www.bls.gov/wsp/data.htm.

[158] Stanley Aronowitz, From the Ashes of the Old: American Labor and America's Future, Houghton Mifflin, chapter 1, p. 44.

[159] Ibid., p. 31f.

[160] A frequently quoted statistic asserts that the cost of loading freight at a dock was $5.86 per ton in the mid-1950s when traditional break bulk methods prevailed versus 16 cents per ton in 1975 using shipping containers loaded onto ships by cranes. It is difficult to verify the accuracy of the comparison and the accounting of costs incurred upstream in packing containers, but even if they achieved only a ten-to-one savings, the dockworkers were under tremendous economic pressure to make some arrangement with shippers.

[161] Ibid., p. 39.

[162] Stanley Aronowitz, "Marxism, Technology, and Labor," *New Political Science*, Vol. 1, Issue 2-3, 1979, p. 105.

[163] Lewis F. Powell, Jr., *Confidential Memorandum: Attack on American Free Enterprise*, Aug. 23, 1971 at http://law.wlu.edu /deptimages/Powell%20Archives/PowellMemorandumTypescript.pdf, p. 17.

[164] Ibid., p. 2.

[165] Ibid., [p. 5, quoting *Richmond Times Dispatch*, July 7, 1971.

[166] Ibid., p. 6.

[167] Ibid., p. 5.

[168] Jacob S. Hacker and Paul Pierson, *Winner-Take-All Politics*, New York, Simon & Schuster, 2010, p. 118.

[169] Henry S. Farber and Bruce Western, "Ronald Reagan and the Politics of Declining Union Organization," Working Paper #460, Industrial Relations Section, Princeton University, Dec. 2001, p. 3.

[170] V. I. Lenin, "Report On The Work Of The Council Of People's Commissars," Dec. 22, 1920, Eighth All-Russia Congress of Soviets, Part II.

[171] "Traditional Society And Culture" in Robert L. Worden, Andrea Matles Savada and Ronald E. Dolan, eds., *China: A Country Study*. Washington, GPO for the Library of Congress, 1987 at http://countrystudies.us/china/42.htm.

[172] Upon crushing the Commune, the bourgeoisie killed an estimated 20,000 to 40,000 Parisians in a week. More died in transport to French prison colonies. Socialist uprising is serious; the people defeat the bourgeoisie or the bourgeoisie slaughters the people.

[173] "Long before me, bourgeois historians had described the historical development of this struggle between the classes, as had bourgeois economists their economic anatomy. My own contribution was 1. to show that the existence of classes is merely bound up with certain historical phases in the development of production; 2. that the class struggle necessarily leads to the dictatorship of the proletariat; 3. that this dictatorship itself constitutes no more than a transition to the abolition of all classes and to a classless society." Karl Marx to J. Weydemeyer, March 5, 1852 at http://www.marxists.org /archive/marx/works/1852/letters/52_03_05.htm. See his analysis of the Commune in *The Civil War in France*. Every class society, including capitalism, is a dictatorship of a class or allied classes over other classes. It is no paradox that capitalist class rule includes formally democratic institutions like elections and a Congress. Their hollowing out reflects the narrower basis of capitalist rule today.

[174] British War Cabinet, Joint Planning Staff, "Operation Unthinkable: 'Russia: Threat to Western Civilization,'" May 22, 1945, p. 1 at http://web.archive.org/web /20101116152301/http://www.history.neu.edu/PRO2/.

[175] Douglas Johnson, "Exit de Gaulle," *History Today*, 49: 4, 1999 at http://www.historytoday.com/douglas-johnson/ exit-de-gaulle.

[176] Ch. 2.

Notes

[177] Commission of the Central Committee of the C.P.S.U. (B.), New York, International, 1939, p. 186.

[178] Andrews, op cit, p. 152.

[179] The topic of individual reward is discussed in chapters nine and ten of Charles Andrews, *From Capitalism to Equality*, Oakland, Needle, 2000.

[180] Left Unity, *Constitution*, p. 1 at http://leftunity.org/wp-content/uploads/2013/12/Constitution-as-of-7-12-13.pdf.

[181] Left Unity, "Statement one," Founding Statements, Nov. 30, 2013, point 3 at http://leftunity.org/founding-conference-decisions-1/.

[182] ISO Educ. Dept., *Where We Stand*, International Socialist Organization, 2009, p. 4 at http://www.internationalsocialist .org/pdfs/WhereWeStandPamphlet.pdf. In words omitted at our ellipsis, the statement says, "Such a society would have no need for a special body to coerce the population – a state – on behalf of a minority exploiting class." The confusion of socialism with the further-off communist era when a state is not needed is anarchism. However, remarks later in the pamphlet override the sentence, indicating an unsettled view.

[183] The Internationale, U.S. version.

[184] Ibid.